NETWORKING WINDOWS FOR WORKGROUPS

NETWORKING WINDOWS FOR WORKGROUPS

Marty Matthews
Bruce Dobson

Osborne **McGraw-Hill**

Berkeley New York St. Louis San Francisco
Auckland Bogotá Hamburg London Madrid
Mexico City Milan Montreal New Delhi Panama City
Paris São Paulo Singapore Sydney
Tokyo Toronto

Osborne **McGraw-Hill**
2600 Tenth Street
Berkeley, California 94710
U.S.A.

For information on translations or book distributors outside of the
U.S.A., please write to Osborne **McGraw-Hill** at the above address.

Networking Windows for Workgroups

Copyright © 1993 by Martin S. Matthews and Carole Boggs Matthews.
All rights reserved. Printed in the United States of America. Except as
permitted under the Copyright Act of 1976, no part of this publication
may be reproduced or distributed in any form or by any means, or
stored in a database or retrieval system, without the prior written
permission of the publisher, with the exception that the program
listings may be entered, stored, and executed in a computer system, but
they may not be reproduced for publication.

1234567890 DOC 99876543

ISBN 0-07-881937-7

Publisher
Kenna S. Wood

Acquisition Editor
Jeffrey M. Pepper

Associate Editor
Emily Rader

Technical Editor
Nick DiMuria

Project Editor
Mark S. Karmendy

Copy Editor
Judith Brown

Proofreader
Mick Arellano

Indexer
Matthew Spence

Illustrator
Marla J. Shelasky

Computer Designer
Marcela Hancik

Cover Designer
Compass Marketing

Information has been obtained by Osborne **McGraw-Hill** from sources believed to be reliable. However, because of the
possibility of human or mechanical error by our sources, Osborne **McGraw-Hill**, or others, Osborne **McGraw-Hill**
does not guarantee the accuracy, adequacy, or completeness of any information and is not responsible for any errors or
omissions or the results obtained from use of such information.

CONTENTS AT A GLANCE

1. Networking Overview 1
2. The Windows Environment 19
3. Selecting and Installing Network Hardware 59
4. Installing and Configuring Windows for Workgroups 83
5. Sharing Your Resources with the Workgroup 119
6. Connecting to the Workgroup Resources 143
7. Using Windows for Workgroups' Mail 165
8. Using Windows for Workgroups' Schedule+ and Other Accessories 205

Index 251

CONTENTS

Acknowledgments xv
Introduction xvii

1 Networking Overview 1
What Is Networking? 2
Types of Networks 3
    Client-Server LANs 4
    Peer-to-Peer LANs 6
Benefits of Networking 7
    Sharing Hardware Resources 7
    Sharing Software Resources 9
Parts of a Network 11
    Computers on a Network 11
    Network Interface Cards 13
    Network Cables 14
    Network Operating Systems 16

2 The Windows Environment 19
Introducing Windows 20
The Windows Screen 22
Using the Mouse 24
    Mousing Around 25

Using Windows 28
    Using Scroll Bars 31
    Starting Applications 33
Using Menus 38
    Using Dialog Boxes 39
Using the Keyboard 41
    Using the Control Menu 43
Using the Main Group Applications 46
    Setting Defaults with the Control Panel 47
    Using the File Manager 50
    Using the ClipBook Viewer 52
Getting Help 55
Leaving Windows 57

3 ▅▅▅ Selecting and Installing Network Hardware 59

Planning Your LAN 60
Network Topologies 64
    Bus Topology 64
    Star Topology 64
    Topology Summary 65
Network Cables 65
    Coaxial Cable 65
    Twisted-Pair Cable 66
Network Interface Cards 68
    Expansion Slots 68
    Ethernet Cards 69
    ARCnet Cards 70
Network Card Settings 70
    Interrupt Request Line 72
    Base I/O Port Address 72
    Base Memory Address 74
    Node Address 76
    Determining Card Settings 76
A Network Shopping List 77
Installing Your Network Hardware 78
Troubleshooting Your Network Hardware 79

4 Installing and Configuring Windows for Workgroups 83

Requirements for Running Windows for
Workgroups 84
Running Windows for Workgroups Setup 86
Tasks Performed by Setup 86
Choosing Your Setup Method 89
Installing Windows for Workgroups with
Setup 93
Starting Windows for Workgroups 95
Standard or 386 Enhanced Mode 95
Specifying a Windows for Workgroups
Mode 96
Starting an Application Automatically 96
Logging on to Windows for Workgroups 97
Customizing Network Settings 99
Changing Your Computer Name 99
Changing Your Workgroup 100
Adding a Comment 100
Enabling and Disabling Sharing 100
Adjusting Performance Priority 100
Changing Logon Settings 101
Additional Options 101
Troubleshooting Windows for Workgroups 102
Read SETUP.TXT 102
Your Network Hardware Does Not Work 103
Your Computer Locks Up in the First Part of
Setup 106
Setup Stops After Completing the First Part 107
Setup Keeps Asking for the Same Floppy
Disk 108
A Hardware Device Doesn't Work 108
Setup Warns You About a Memory-Resident
Program 109
Windows Won't Start After Setup Finishes 109
You Can Run in Standard but Not 386
Enhanced Mode 110

Problems with Network Features 111
Problems with Your Mouse 114
Copying a File from a Windows Setup Disk 115
For Further Help 116

5 ▇▇▇ Sharing Your Resources with the Workgroup 119

What Does Sharing Your Resources Mean? 120
Shared Directory and Printer Paths 121
Sharing Directories and Closing Files with File
   Manager 122
   Sharing a Disk Directory 122
   Displaying Users and Closing Files 125
   Changing Access to Your Shared
     Directories 128
Using the Print Manager to Share a Printer 129
   Designating a Printer as Shared 130
   Viewing and Canceling Document Printing 133
   Changing Access to Your Shared Printer 134
Using the ClipBook Viewer to Share Local
   ClipBook Pages 135
   Moving Information onto the Clipboard 135
   Pasting the Clipboard Contents into Your
     Local ClipBook 136
   Changing Access to Your Shared ClipBook
     Page 140
Stopping the Sharing of All Your Resources 141

6 ▇▇▇ Connecting to the Workgroup Resources 143

Using Shared Directories 144
   Reserving Drive Letters with the LASTDRIVE
     Command 144
   Browsing and Connecting to a Shared
     Directory 145
   Disconnecting from a Shared Directory 149
Using Shared Printers 150
   Connecting to a Network Printer 150

Setting Up a Network Printer 154
Disconnecting from a Network Printer 156
Using Shared ClipBook Pages 156
Introduction to the ClipBook Viewer 156
Connecting to a Shared ClipBook Page 158
Disconnecting from a Shared ClipBook 160
Using the Information on ClipBook Pages 160

7 Using Windows for Workgroups' Mail 165

Introducing Mail 166
The Workgroup Postoffice 166
Your Personal Mailbox 167
Mail Help 167
Getting Started 169
Starting Mail for the First Time 170
Connecting to the Postoffice 170
Opening a Personal Mailbox 172
Signing In 173
Using the Address Book 174
Entering and Sending Your Message 177
Receiving Mail 179
Reading Your Mail 179
Replying to Mail 180
Forwarding Mail 181
Housekeeping 183
Filing Mail 183
Creating Address Groups 185
Finding Mail 186
Deleting Mail 187
Printing Messages 188
Quitting Mail 188
Creating Mail Templates 188
Working with Mail Offline 189
Attaching Files to Mail 189
Object Embedding with Mail 191
The Workgroup Postoffice Administrator 192
Setting Up the Workgroup Postoffice 193

Setting Up the Postoffice Administration
Account 193
Sharing the Workgroup Postoffice 194
Setting Up Individual Accounts 195
Maintaining the Postoffice Files 197
Other Networks and Mail 200
Novell's NetWare 201
Microsoft's LAN Manager 201
Other Networks 201
Troubleshooting 201

8 ■■■ Using Windows for Workgroups' Schedule+ and Other Accessories 205

Introducing Schedule+ 206
Your Appointment Book 206
The Task List 207
The Planner 208
Arranging Meetings 208
Schedule+ Help 209
Using Your Appointment Book 211
Changing Defaults 213
Adding Appointments 214
Recurring Appointments 219
Adding a Tentative Appointment 221
Setting Reminders 221
Quitting Schedule+ 222
Using the Task List 223
Adding Tasks 223
Modifying Tasks 228
Integrating Tasks with Your Appointment
Book 231
Printing Your Appointment Book and Task List 233
Sharing Schedule+ 234
Providing Access to Others 234
Gaining Access to Other Users' Schedules 237
Using Other Scheduling Programs 238
Using Schedule+ to Arrange Meetings 240

Using an Assistant 242
Scheduling Resources 243
Using Chat 244
Net Watcher 247
WinMeter 249

Index **251**

ACKNOWLEDGMENTS

John Cronan broke into the ranks of writers in this book and did so in grand style. John jumped in with short notice to write Chapters 7 and 8 and did an excellent job on time—a great way to start a career.

Emily Rader and Judith Brown did a superb job of editing the manuscript on a very tight schedule. Their efforts are greatly appreciated.

Bruce wishes to thank his wife Jane for putting up with the long hours and weekends it took to finish this book. Without her understanding and support this project would not have been possible.

Marty wishes to thank his wife Carole and his son Michael for their love and support. Not only did they make doing the book possible, they also make it worthwhile.

INTRODUCTION

Windows for Workgroups is a breakthrough in user-friendly networking. The easy-to-use graphical user interface of Windows now includes built-in networking capabilities. It is ideally suited for smaller workgroups that need to share information without using the "sneakernet" method of passing floppy disks back and forth. With Windows for Workgroups you can send electronic mail and documents to each other, schedule your meetings and appointments, share printers and other devices, and share the software on your disks.

A Windows for Workgroups network can be installed and maintained by your workgroup members, and does not require anyone to act as a network administrator. If anyone in your workgroup feels comfortable taking the covers off computers, plugging in cards, and running cables between desks, then you probably have the hardware installation covered. The Setup program that comes with Windows for Workgroups makes installing the software quite painless, and should take less than an hour of your time.

About This Book

Networking Windows for Workgroups is the one book you need to set up and use a network with Windows for Workgroups. This book guides you through the selection and installation of your network hardware, tells you what you need to know about setting up Windows for

Workgroups, including optimizing it for your computer, and provides help in dealing with the many problems that could occur during installation. The book then goes on to show you how to fully integrate Windows for Workgroups in your organization, pointing out the many practical uses and benefits of networking.

How This Book Is Organized

Networking Windows for Workgroups is organized the way most people learn to use a new product. The book begins by reviewing the basic concepts of networking and Windows. It then guides you in the step-by-step process of designing, selecting, and installing your network hardware and then installing and optimizing Windows for Workgroups itself. Next, *Networking Windows for Workgroups* uses a learn-by-doing approach to demonstrate the sharing and utilizing of the group's resources, which is at the heart of networking. Finally, the book concludes with in-depth explorations of the Mail and Schedule+ applications that are included with Windows for Workgroups.

Overview of Networking and Windows

Chapters 1 and 2 provide an overview of networking and Windows. Chapter 1 introduces networking by describing what it is, what you can do with it, the types of networks that are available, and the components in a network and their functions. Chapter 2 introduces Windows and discusses the windows screen and its components, menus and dialog boxes, using the mouse, starting and switching applications, and how to get help.

Network Design and Installation

Chapters 3 and 4 cover the design, installation, and setup of a network using Windows for Workgroups. Chapter 3 explores the various types of network adapter cards, cabling, and options that are available and usable with Windows for Workgroups. The pros and cons of each option are discussed and recommendations are made. Parts lists are provided as are tables of the appropriate settings. A complete step-by-step procedure for installing a network followed by a troubleshooting guide complete the chapter.

Introduction

Chapter 4 covers the process of installing Windows for Workgroups in detail. It then goes into how to configure, customize, and optimize Windows for Workgroups to fit your needs. Various options are discussed and recommendations are provided. An extensive troubleshooting section concludes the chapter.

Sharing and Connecting to Resources

Chapters 5 and 6 provide a basic guide on how to most beneficially use a Windows for Workgroups network. Chapter 5 looks at what resources on your computer should be made available to the other members of the workgroup and how to do that. The steps for sharing disks, directories, printers, and ClipBook pages are covered.

Chapter 6 describes how to connect your computer to the resources that are available on the network. It covers the techniques for connecting to disks, directories, printers, and ClipBook pages.

Using Mail and Schedule+

Chapters 7 and 8 look at two new applications included with Windows for Workgroups. Chapter 7 discusses Windows for Workgroups' Mail and how to set up and run a "Postoffice." Using mailboxes and passwords is discussed as well as creating, sending, reading, and deleting messages; attaching files and managing disk space; and troubleshooting problems in Mail.

Chapter 8 discusses Windows for Workgroups' Schedule+ and how to set up and use the Appointment Book, task list, and Planner. You learn how to jointly schedule meetings among workgroup members and how to tie Mail messages to Schedule+. The chapter concludes with a discussion of the new accessories: Chat, Net Watcher, and WinMeter, along with suggestions for getting the most out of them.

Conventions Used in This Book

Networking Windows for Workgroups uses several conventions designed to make the book easier for you to read. These are as follows:

♦ **Bold** type is used for text you are instructed to type from the keyboard.

Networking Windows for Workgroups

◆ Keys on the keyboard are presented in key-shaped boxes; for example, [Tab] and [Enter].

◆ When you are expected to enter a command, you are told to *press* the key(s). If you are to enter text or numbers, you are told to *type* them.

CHAPTER

1

NETWORKING OVERVIEW

Computer networks are transforming the personal computer world. Personal computers have traditionally been isolated, stand-alone units, but when networked they become interconnected, communicating parts of larger systems. This connectedness gives each user access to resources and communication tools not available with purely personal *computers. In fact, these computers are typically called "desktop" rather than "personal" computers now, which reflects their less isolated nature.*

In this chapter you learn what networking is, what you can do with a network, what the parts of a network are, and how Windows for Workgroups fits into the networking picture. If you are currently a Windows user, you will recognize the familiar Windows environment in Windows for Workgroups. With the networking capabilities built into it, Windows for Workgroups makes networking your workgroup easier than it has ever been. If your networking needs include sharing resources and communicating among two to ten users, Windows for Workgroups is your ideal networking solution.

What Is Networking?

The quick definition of a network is two or more computers connected together in order to exchange data and share resources. These resources include printers, disk space, application software, documents, databases, fax machines, and modems. Figure 1-1 shows a small network that shares a printer and a modem. The computers in a network have special network boards installed in them, they are connected by cables (that contain the wires over which messages travel), and they run software that enables them to communicate.

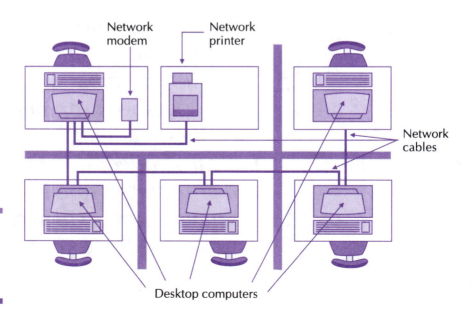

A small network with shared printer and modem
Figure 1-1.

Networking Overview

Networking includes more than just increasing the resources available to each user. The connectedness of the computers on a network enables users to communicate and share information more easily, and in new ways. For example, a network enables members of a *workgroup* (a group of people who work together) to coordinate their schedules, send electronic mail to each other, and share the editing of documents. A new class of networking software designed exclusively for use by workgroups, called *groupware,* has become available, and is discussed later in this chapter. Many popular software applications are available in network versions, allowing multiple users to run them and modify data files simultaneously.

Types of Networks

A network can consist of two computers sitting side by side on a desk, a large number of computers located in widely separated parts of the world, or anything in between these two extremes. Most networks fall into either of two general classes: wide area or local area networks.

A *wide area network* (WAN) connects computers or other networks located across town or thousands of miles apart. WANs use telephone, satellite, microwave, or other transmission methods to carry the messages between them. WANs are highly complex networks administered by professionals, and are beyond the scope of this book.

The most popular type of network, and the type that this book covers, is the *local area network* (LAN). The computers in a LAN are located fairly close together, typically in the same office or building, and are connected directly by cables (except for the new wireless LANs, discussed later in this chapter).

It is important to distinguish between a LAN and a multiuser system like those typically found with mainframe and minicomputer systems. A *multiuser system* consists of one powerful computer to which a number of terminals are connected. *Terminals* usually consist of a keyboard and monitor, with little or no processing power of their own. The main computer does all the work for the users, running applications for all of the terminals simultaneously. The terminals in these systems are simply input and output stations, and if the central processor goes down the whole system stops working. Figure 1-2 shows a small multiuser system.

4

Networking Windows for Workgroups

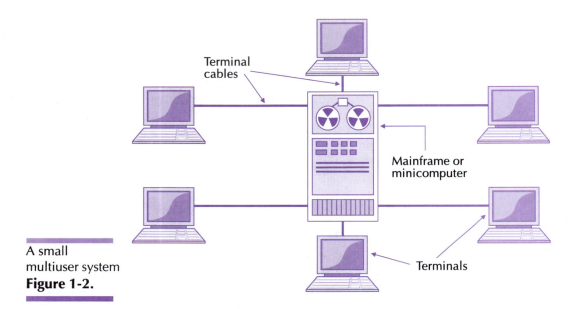

A small multiuser system
Figure 1-2.

A LAN is like a multiuser system in the way it enables multiple connected users to work simultaneously at different tasks while sharing resources and communicating among themselves. The principal difference is that the computers connected to a LAN are capable of running their own applications rather than relying on one central computer to do this for them. This decentralization of processing power is called *distributed processing*. It is a more stable system than the centralized systems, since the individual computers are usually capable of working as stand-alone systems if the network goes down.

LANs differ among themselves in the degree to which they distribute networking tasks, and fall into two broad design categories: client-server and peer-to-peer.

Client-Server LANs

The earliest LANs and most large LANs today (LANs with ten or more users) are *client-server* LANs. In a client-server LAN, each connected computer is either a *server*, which carries most of the workload, or *client*, which uses the resources provided by the server(s). Typically, a

Networking Overview

client-server LAN has one server and multiple client computers. Figure 1-3 shows a simple client-server LAN.

The server manages network files, controls the network printers and other peripherals connected to it, and manages the network communications. A server is usually entirely dedicated to performing its server tasks and cannot be used to run end-user applications (like word processors or spreadsheets). The computer that functions as a server on these LANs must be powerful enough to handle simultaneous requests from clients, and is often a specially designed server machine.

The clients, or *workstations,* are those desktop computers on which users perform productive work, and are typically less powerful than the server. A client might even lack its own hard disk drive, depending entirely on the server for disk functions. However, clients must be capable of running their own applications. They are usually ordinary desktop computers with hard disks and sometimes a local printer attached.

Examples of client-server networking software include Novell NetWare and Microsoft LAN Manager.

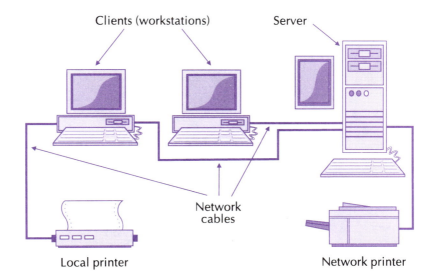

A simple client-server network
Figure 1-3.

Peer-to-Peer LANs

Most smaller networks are *peer-to-peer* networks. Windows for Workgroups supports this type of network. Peer-to-peer network design distributes the networking tasks more evenly among the connected computers, because each computer (or *node*) in a peer-to-peer network can function as both a server and a client. This means that each node on the LAN can share its resources with every other node on the LAN. For example, any node on a peer-to-peer LAN can share an application or data file stored on its hard disk, or a printer connected to it. Figure 1-4 shows a typical peer-to-peer network.

The peer-to-peer arrangement is particularly well suited to setting up an inexpensive network with a small group of computers, since each computer is likely to have adequate hardware and no powerful server needs to be purchased. Each computer in such a workgroup can continue to be used in the usual way as a stand-alone machine. At the same time, it can share the files on its hard disk with others or send print jobs to printers connected to other computers.

The network software for peer-to-peer LANs is much less expensive than that for the larger server-based LANs, and it runs as a memory-resident program under DOS. (A *memory-resident* program is

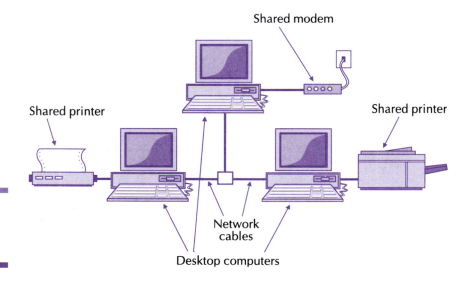

A small peer-to-peer network
Figure 1-4.

Networking Overview

one that, once started, continues to run in the background while you run other "foreground" applications.) Since the computer is still running DOS, all of the software that normally runs on it will still be able to run after the network is installed. The installation and maintenance of peer-to-peer software is also much simpler than that of client-server systems. As you will discover, Windows for Workgroups is very easy to set up and maintain.

Benefits of Networking

The benefits of networking your desktop computers fall into three general categories:

- Better utilization of hardware resources
- Sharing and controlling software resources
- Enhancing communication among users

A Windows for Workgroups network can realize most of the benefits discussed here. Bear in mind that the word *server,* when applied to a peer-to-peer LAN, refers to any computer that can share its resources with others.

Sharing Hardware Resources

Often the primary motivation for installing a network is to share an expensive hardware device, such as a high-resolution laser printer, a sophisticated plotter, or a large and fast hard drive. When an expensive device is shared by several users, the cost per user is reduced at the same time as the amount of resources available to each user is increased. Besides printers, plotters, and hard disks, hardware devices typically shared include high-speed modems, fax machines, and compact disk read-only memory (CD-ROM) drives.

Printers

A printing device can be shared easily by the users on a network by connecting it to a server computer. Users can then send their print jobs to that printer, rather than the one (if any) attached to their own computer. This arrangement enables everyone on the network to share a high-quality laser printer, for example, while avoiding the expense of buying one for each user.

While sharing a printer appears to be the ideal way to reduce costs and improve productivity, there are some disadvantages. Users must retrieve their printouts from the shared printer, which might be an inconvenient distance away. Unless the printer is capable of automatically selecting different types of paper, users might have to make an additional trip to the printer to load the correct type of paper for the print job. An additional consideration is the heavy use a shared printer might experience, which could necessitate the purchase of a heavy-duty model. Despite these drawbacks, the sharing of printers is one of the primary motivations for installing small LANs.

Hard Disks

Networking software allows users to store their data on a server's hard disk, assign it a drive letter, and access it in the same way that they access their *local* drive (one that exists on their own computer). This is an important benefit of networking, since large hard drives are expensive, and the amount of hard disk space needed by different users varies widely. Some users never seem to have enough hard disk space, while others prefer to keep files on floppy disks, and do not need a large hard disk. When a large amount of hard disk space on a server is available to those who need it, the sizes of other hard drives on the LAN can be modest.

There are also security benefits to storing user files on a server's hard drive: access to the hard drive's directories can usually be restricted to certain authorized persons, and backups (copying hard disk files to another media like floppies or magnetic tape) can be accomplished easily using a single backup system.

Modems and Fax Boards

With network versions of communication software, you can share modems and fax boards on a LAN. Although modems and fax boards are available at relatively low prices, the faster modems can be expensive. However, the expense of adding phone lines for individual users (or tying up existing phone lines with data transmission) may be the biggest factor in deciding whether sharing modems and fax boards makes economic sense.

Networking Overview

CD-ROM Drives

The growing amount of information available on CD-ROM disks (each disk holds up to 650MB), and decreasing prices for the drives that read those disks, make sharing this type of device practical. If your workgroup needs information that is available on CD-ROM disks, you might find it cost-effective to share a CD-ROM drive. These drives can be shared in the same way that hard disks are shared.

Sharing Software Resources

Because hard disks can be shared on a LAN, many options for sharing the files stored on the disks also exist. Although many small LANs exist simply to share hardware resources, sharing application software or data will most likely benefit your workgroup. One benefit of sharing data files or documents is the elimination of the "sneakernet" method of sharing files by passing floppy disks back and forth. Types of software that LANs allow you to share include single-user or network versions of applications (including database applications), documents or data files, and groupware applications. Each of these is discussed next.

Single-User Software

Single-user software is the application software designed to be used by one person on one computer at a time. When you connect your computers to form a network, you can still run most single-user software on the individual workstations, as before. Some single-user applications can be shared successfully on a LAN, but others will fail in various ways. You should verify the compatibility of any single-user software that you plan to share.

If you want to conserve hard disk space by sharing one copy of a single-user application, be aware that most software licenses for this type of software require you to purchase copies for every user, even if you use only one copy. If a network version of the software is available, consider purchasing it for better performance and to avoid legal problems.

LAN Software

Many popular applications are available in LAN (or network or server) editions. These LAN products are designed to be run by multiple users simultaneously and to avoid the problems associated with running single-user software on a LAN. The licensing requirements vary from product to product, but for smaller networks you typically purchase a license to use the software based on the maximum number of people that can simultaneously use the product. Sometimes the licensing agreements are only available in increments of 5-, 10-, and 20-user versions, so you might pay more for the LAN version than the correct number of single-user copies. Another variable to consider is whether multiple copies of the reference manual are provided with LAN versions.

Shared Databases   Using a database on a LAN can greatly enhance workgroup productivity by allowing several users to access the database simultaneously. While a single-user database application may suffice if just one person will be using it at any time, a LAN version of the application allows simultaneous changes to be made without danger of corruption or loss of data. For some businesses, this simultaneous access to a large database is the primary reason for having a LAN.

Groupware

Networks are particularly well suited for workgroups. A workgroup could be a department in a company, the members of a project team, or an entire office. Members of a workgroup typically need to communicate among themselves and share files and other resources.

Groupware (sometimes called network productivity software) is software developed with the needs of workgroups in mind, and it exists only on LANs. Groupware like Windows for Workgroups is intended to make a workgroup more productive by facilitating communication and interaction among its members. It typically includes the following features. (Windows for Workgroups includes all of these features.)

✦ **Scheduling** Scheduling (or calendaring) software provides each user with a personal appointment calendar in which appointments and meetings can be scheduled and personal notes can be recorded. There is usually a notification option included, which can remind you in advance of any event or appointment. The personal calendar can be shared with another person or kept private.

The group calendaring part of this software allows workgroup members to view the open times in the schedules of others and to

Networking Overview

schedule meetings in these blocks. The details of these appointments are then automatically added to the appropriate members' calendars. Regularly scheduled meetings appear in everyone's schedules in advance, so conflicts are minimized. Of course, workgroup members must reserve blocks of time for themselves in order to control when others can claim their time.

✦ **Electronic mail** This type of software is popularly known as *e-mail*, and it enables workgroup members to send and receive electronic messages and files. These electronic data packages are typically stored on a shared disk in *encrypted* (scrambled) form, and they are not readable by anyone who does not know the user's password. Messages are held until the group member reads his or her mail by running the e-mail program. Some e-mail software can notify users when they receive mail.

E-mail software often includes the capability to send messages to a specified list of people, attach any type of file to a message, maintain an audit trail of messages, and print messages. While it does not eliminate the use of paper in the office, e-mail can help reduce the amount that is needlessly wasted.

✦ **Utilities** Groupware typically includes several handy desktop utilities such as a calculator, phone number card file, text editor, file manager, screen savers, and sometimes games. When groupware includes these utilities, the need to purchase and run separate applications for these tasks is reduced or eliminated.

Parts of a Network

A network consists of both hardware (computers, network cards, cables) and the network operating system running on the computers. These are discussed next.

Computers on a Network

As you learned earlier, desktop computers on a LAN are sometimes classified according to their LAN functions: servers or clients (workstations). On large LANs that experience heavy network loads, the computers are specialized. They typically have one or two powerful servers and many slower (and less expensive) workstations.

Servers

Servers on large LANs are usually dedicated exclusively to network functions such as processing requests from workstations for file services, servicing the network printers and queues, and handling various other communication requests from workstations. The demands on a server increase as the number of workstations logged on to the network increases. If the number of requests is higher than the server can receive, process, and respond to in a short time, the workstations resend their requests, adding to the congestion. Server computers must be powerful enough to keep up with this kind of network traffic. They usually have large, fast hard drives and plenty of random access memory (RAM). The cost of a dedicated file server appropriate for a large LAN, with a 486 processor running at 33 MHz or faster, 16MB of memory, a gigabyte (1,024MB) of fast hard drive storage, and other speed-enhancing features, can exceed $10,000.

Client Workstations

The workstations on client-server LANs have about the same hardware requirements as stand-alone desktop computers. They are usually less powerful machines than a server. Occasionally a workstation is more powerful than the server because of the type of application it runs—computer-aided design (CAD) software, for example. But this is the exception. Since workstations can use the files on the server's hard drive as if they were on their own drive, they need not be equipped with hard drives. In fact, workstations sometimes don't even have a floppy drive. This helps prevent the introduction of viruses and unauthorized software onto the server, and it prevents the copying of sensitive data onto floppy disks.

Peer-to-Peer Workstations

The hardware requirements for computers on a peer-to-peer LAN fall somewhere in between those for servers and workstations on a client-server LAN. Since every node on a peer-to-peer LAN can function

Networking Overview

as both a server and a workstation, the workload is spread out. This eliminates the need to purchase an expensive computer that devotes all its power to supporting the LAN. However, it also means that each computer must be equipped with a hard drive and have enough power to share its resources with others, while continuing to run its own application(s) at a reasonable pace.

Each node on a peer-to-peer LAN is an ordinary desktop computer typically equipped with a hard drive and one or two floppy drives, and can function as either a stand-alone or a networked computer. Windows for Workgroups requires that the computers on your LAN be capable of running in standard mode at a minimum, which requires an 80286 or newer processor. In order to share resources, however, they must be capable of running in 386 enhanced mode, which requires an 80386 or newer processor. See Chapter 4 for more information on the minimum requirements for running Windows for Workgroups.

NOTE: To use Windows for Workgroups you do not need to decide whether each computer is a client or server (or both). In fact, these terms are not used at all. When Windows for Workgroups refers to a computer sharing its resources with others it implies that the computer is acting as a server, and when it refers to a computer connecting to the resources of others it implies that the computer is acting as a client.

Network Interface Cards

Each computer on the LAN has a network interface card plugged into a slot on its motherboard. The *network interface card* (also called a LAN card, network interface unit, network board, and LAN adapter) provides the connector for the cables that run between the computers on the LAN, and generates the electrical signals that carry messages. Figure 1-5 shows a typical network interface card. Network cards usually have jumpers and switches on them, and part of the installation process involves setting these jumpers and switches to make the card compatible with the computer that it is going into. Chapter 3 covers various types of network interface cards in detail, helps you decide

Network
interface card
Figure 1-5.

which type is appropriate for your particular needs, and shows you how to configure it.

Network Cables

The nodes on most LANs are connected by cables. The new wireless LANs are an exception—they use radio or infrared signals instead of cables to carry information between computers. The way these cables are actually connected is called the *topology* of the LAN, and most small LANs use one of the following schemes:

✦ **Bus** This is the simplest topology and the one most often used for small LANs with six or fewer nodes. The bus is formed by running individual cables from one node to the next node to form a line of connected computers. This way of connecting computers is also known as *daisy-chaining,* and is shown in Figure 1-6.

✦ **Star** This topology uses a central hub with cables radiating out to the individual nodes on the LAN, as shown in Figure 1-7. Star topology has some advantages over bus topology: failure of a cable usually brings down only one node, and it is sometimes easier to

Networking Overview

expand or reconfigure the LAN since two stars can be connected to each other.

✦ **Ring** This third scheme forms the connected nodes into a closed loop. Rings use more expensive electronics and are not generally used for small LANs.

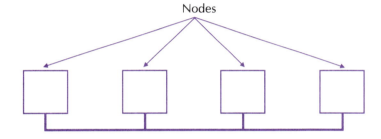

Bus topology, usually used for small LANs of six or fewer nodes
Figure 1-6.

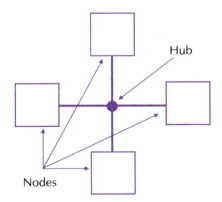

Star topology uses a central hub with cables radiating out to the individual nodes on the LAN
Figure 1-7.

Network Operating Systems

The software that enables the LAN nodes to actually communicate is called the *network operating system,* or sometimes, network software or the LAN operating system. The network operating system is what makes a LAN a client-server or peer-to-peer network. Some network operating systems completely replace DOS, while others ride "on top of" DOS, adding the communication capabilities that DOS lacks. Following is a brief discussion of the two general types of network operating systems, which correspond to the client-server and peer-to-peer types of LANs.

Client-Server Operating Systems

Larger LANs generally use the client-server approach to networking. This design uses one computer (the server) as the center of the network, with the rest of the computers (the workstations, or clients) connected to it and relying on it for network files and other resources. The central server is often not available for anything except serving the workstations. The server typically runs a special network operating system instead of DOS and has a specially formatted hard drive. The special network operating system on such systems allows them to perform their server functions much faster than would be possible with DOS.

The workstations on client-server LANs usually run DOS. They load software that links to the network hardware and includes a program called a *shell*, which allows them to interface with the network operating system. In order to gain access to the files on the server's hard drive, the user at a workstation must log on to the network. One of the strengths of the server-based type of network operating system is the high degree of control over who can log on to the server (and when), which directories users are allowed access to, and which operations they are allowed to perform on the files.

Client-server network operating systems can be complicated and time-consuming to install, requiring customization of each computer's software based on the particular network hardware installed and the computer's function in the LAN. This type of LAN requires a knowledgeable person to act as the supervisor, or network administrator, who takes charge of such tasks as creating and deleting user accounts, setting the access restrictions for each user, and monitoring the state of the network.

Networking Overview

Peer-to-Peer Operating Systems

Peer-to-Peer network operating systems are designed to be decentralized and to make the most of the computing resources of a relatively small group of users. Each node in this type of LAN can share its own resources with all the other nodes. It must have enough power to run an application for its own user while simultaneously providing some service for another user on the LAN.

The network operating system for a peer-to-peer LAN typically runs on top of DOS as a memory-resident program that adds the ability to communicate with other computers on the LAN. In contrast to client-server software, peer-to-peer software is designed to be easy to install and maintain by nonexperts. Installation of an individual node's portion of the network software takes about 30 minutes or less and involves answering a few questions posed by the installation program. Some peer-to-peer systems ask you to decide whether the node is being set up as a server, workstation, or both. The appropriate software is then set up on the computer's hard disk. Workstation software takes up a small amount of disk space and memory; server software uses a bit more.

Windows for Workgroups is a peer-to-peer network operating system, is no more difficult to install than Windows, and takes very little more memory or disk space. Peer-to-peer network operating systems, including Windows for Workgroups, are usually sold on a per-node basis, so you only pay for what you need. For a small number of nodes—not more than ten—a peer-to-peer system makes sense.

CHAPTER

2

THE WINDOWS ENVIRONMENT

Windows is considered an environment *in contrast to an* operating system *such as* DOS. *Windows provides the interface between you and the applications that run under Windows. This interface includes the way Windows shows you on the screen what it is doing, and the way you tell Windows what to do. This chapter introduces you to the essentials of Microsoft Windows for Workgroups. You may never use all of the capabilities and tools available in Windows for Workgroups, but when you* become acquainted with them, you will appreciate the potential that is available in the Windows environment.

This chapter is more of a tutorial than the rest of the book. It proceeds more slowly in order to establish a foundation for using this book. If you are already familiar with Windows and the mouse, simply scan the chapter to verify that you know the terminology used here and the basic operating procedures used in Windows for Workgroups.

Introducing Windows

Windows is an extension of the MS-DOS operating system that offers a standard environment for all of the programs or applications that run under it. This environment consists chiefly of a standard screen display, or *visual interface*, that you use to communicate with Windows applications. Once you learn to use Windows, you will find that working with the various applications that run under Windows is very similar.

Windows also provides a way to transfer information among applications, such as from Excel to Word for Windows or Excel to PageMaker. Through this feature, called the Clipboard, you can easily move a portion of an application document, like an Excel worksheet or an Excel chart, to another application document like a Word for Windows word processing document. In Windows for Workgroups, the Clipboard has been augmented with the ClipBook, which allows you to transfer information within a network and to permanently store items being transferred. See "Using the ClipBook" toward the end of this chapter.

Windows allows you to load more than one application into memory at the same time and to switch among applications with minimal effort. You can work with a word processor, a graphics application, and a spreadsheet all at the same time. Of course, the degree to which this can be done depends on the amount of memory in your computer.

Finally, Windows for Workgroups provides a set of applications that are handy accessories. The icons for these applications are shown here:

The Windows Environment

Three of these accessories, Net Watcher, WinMeter, and Chat are network related and will be discussed in depth in Chapter 9. A brief description of all of the accessories is provided in the following table:

Accessory	Description
Calculator	A program for adding, subtracting, multiplying, and dividing numbers
Cardfile	A list management program similar to using 3-by-5 index cards
Character Map	A table of the available characters in the current font
Chat	A program that allows you to converse with someone else on the network using the keyboard
Clock	An analog or digital clock that can be displayed on the screen
Net Watcher	A program that lets you see who on the network is connected to your computer and lets you disconnect them
Notepad	A program that lets you keep notes, reminders, and other memos handy

Accessory	Description
Media Player	A program to control multi-media hardware and software, such as CD-ROMs and sound boards
Object Packager	A program that lets you embed or link a full or partial document (in the form of an icon) into another document
Paintbrush	A graphics program
Recorder	A means of recording and playing back sets of keystrokes and mouse actions to produce macros
Sound Recorder	A program that lets you play, edit, and record sound files when you have the necessary hardware
Terminal	A communication program that lets you connect via a modem and telephone lines to another computer
WinMeter	A program that graphically shows you the amount of your computer's resources that are being used
Write	A word processing program

In Windows for Workgroups, you have all of these accessories available to you on demand.

The quickest way to learn about Windows for Workgroups is to start using it. If you have not already done so, turn on your computer now and start Windows. If you have not already installed Windows, do so now. When you complete the installation and your mouse is connected, return here.

The Windows Screen

When Windows for Workgroups is started, you first see a screen similar to the one shown in Figure 2-1. (Depending on how you installed Windows and if you have non-Windows applications or other Windows applications, your screen may look different.) The screen in Figure 2-1 shows two windows, both with several standard features that appear in most windows. The top line, or *title bar*, of a window contains its title. The two windows in the figure are the Program Manager

The Windows Environment

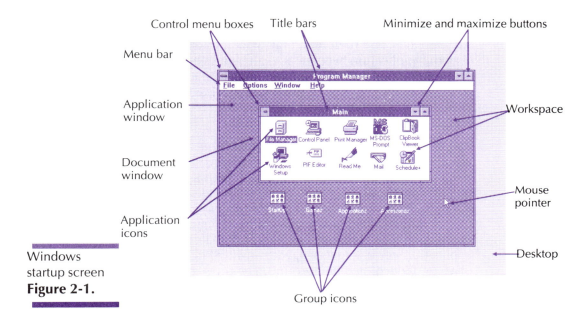

Windows startup screen
Figure 2-1.

application window and the Main group *document window*. The area behind the windows is called the *desktop*.

On the left end of the title bar is the *Control menu box*. You use this box to access the *Control menu*, which contains options that allow you to perform such operations as moving, sizing, or closing a window using the keyboard. On the right end of the title bar are the *minimize* and *maximize* buttons, which are used for changing the size of the window using the mouse.

Below the title bar in the Program Manager window is the *menu bar*. The menus available (File, Options, Window, and Help) apply only to the Program Manager. The menus displayed in the menu bar change as the window changes.

Below the menu bar is the *workspace*, which contains, at the top, the Main group document window. At the bottom of the workspace, as shown in Figure 2-1, are graphic symbols, called *group icons*, that represent four groups of programs you can use. Inside the Main group window are ten *application icons* that represent nine programs and one information file that you can run or read. Double-clicking on an application icon starts that program. When you start an application such as Excel, and then temporarily set it aside while you do something else, the application becomes an icon again, but now it is at the bottom of the screen on the desktop. An application icon on the desktop can be reactivated, moved around the screen, or deactivated. Whatever you were doing in the application remains frozen just as you left it, until it is reactivated or the application is closed.

Several indicators show where you are on the screen. First, the *active window*—the one you are currently working in—is indicated by the color of its title bar and border, usually with light letters on a dark background. Both the Program Manager and Main group windows are active in Figure 2-1. Second, the *selected object* or objects—what your next action will affect—is highlighted. In Figure 2-1 the File Manager application icon is the selected object. You know this because the application name is reversed, with white or light-colored letters on a black or dark-colored background. The third indicator is the *mouse pointer,* which, in this case, is an arrow that tells you where the mouse is pointing. In Figure 2-1 the arrow is in the Program Manager's workspace. All three indicators change as you work. The varying symbols tell you something about the task being done. You'll see examples later.

Using the Mouse

Although Windows allows you to use either the mouse or the keyboard to enter commands, using a mouse will greatly increase the power of Windows for you. Most instructions in this book assume that you are using a mouse. The keyboard occasionally does offer shortcuts, so these shortcuts and some general rules for using the keyboard are covered later in this chapter.

The mouse is used to move the pointer on the screen. You can *select* an object by moving the mouse until the pointer is on top of it (pointing *on* it) and then pressing the mouse button. Using the mouse in this way allows you to choose, for example, an option on a menu. A mouse can have one, two, or three buttons. Normally, Windows uses only one button, called the *mouse button* in this book. By default the left button is used, but you can change the default to another button. You may want to do this if you are left-handed. (You'll see how later in this chapter.)

The Windows Environment

Mousing Around

If you move the mouse across a flat surface such as a table or desk, the mouse pointer (the arrow on the screen) also moves. Practice moving the mouse with these instructions:

1. Place your hand on the mouse. The button(s) should be under your fingers with the cord leading away from you.

2. Move the mouse now, without pressing the mouse button, and watch the pointer move on the screen.

   If you run out of room while moving the mouse, simply pick it up and place it where there is more room. Try experimenting with this now.

3. Move the mouse to the edge of your work surface; then pick it up and place it in the middle of your work surface and move it again.

   Watch how the pointer continues from where the mouse was picked up. When you point on the border of the window, the arrow changes to a double-headed arrow. This tells you that the pointer is on the border. If you press the mouse button here, you can size the window, as you will see shortly.

This book uses the following standard Windows terminology to describe your actions with the mouse:

◆ **Press** Hold down the mouse button.

◆ **Release** Quit pressing the mouse button.

◆ **Point on** Move the mouse until the tip of the pointer is on top of the item you want.

◆ **Click** Quickly press and release the mouse button once.

◆ **Click on** Point on an item and click.

◆ **Double-click** Press and release the mouse button twice in rapid succession.

◆ **Drag** Press and hold the mouse button while you move the mouse (to move the highlight bar within a menu to the desired option, to move an object in the work area, and to highlight contiguous text you want to delete, move, or copy).

◆ **Select** Point on an item and click the mouse button (same as click on).

◆ **Choose** Click on a menu option or drag the pointer (and the corresponding highlight bar) to a menu option and release the mouse button.

Work through the following demonstration of mouse actions, and then you will be able to follow the instructions in this book. For example, the instruction, "Select the File menu and choose the Run option," means that you should point on the word "File" in the menu bar, press and hold the mouse button while moving the mouse toward you to drag the highlight bar down to the Run option, and then release the mouse button.

Practice using the mouse to perform some of these actions:

1. *Point on* the Accessories group icons at the bottom of the Program Manager window by moving the mouse (and the corresponding pointer) until the pointer is resting on it.

2. *Select* the Accessories group icon by *clicking*—quickly pressing and releasing the mouse button while pointing—on it. The title bar beneath the icon is highlighted, indicating it is selected.

3. *Drag* the Accessories group icon to the lower-right corner of the Program Manager window. First point on the icon, then press and hold the mouse button while you move the mouse. Move it until the pointer and the icon are in the lower-right corner of the window, as shown in Figure 2-2.

4. *Drag* the Accessories group icon back to its original position.

5. *Click* on the minimize button—the downward pointing arrow in the upper-right corner of the Main group window. The window closes and becomes another group icon, as shown in Figure 2-3.

6. *Double-click* on the Accessories group icon in the lower part of the Program Manager window. The Accessories window opens, as shown in Figure 2-4.

7. *Double-click* on the Control menu box in the upper-left corner of the Accessories window. The Accessories window closes.

8. *Double-click* on the Accessories icon again to reopen the Accessories window.

The Windows Environment

Dragging a group icon to the lower-right corner
Figure 2-2.

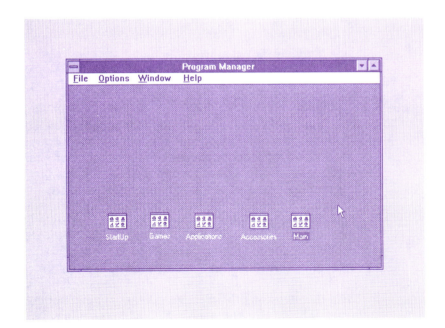

Main group window closed to a group icon
Figure 2-3.

Accessories group window open
Figure 2-4.

It sometimes takes a couple of tries to get the rhythm of double-clicking. A frequent problem is double-clicking too slowly. You will see later in this chapter how you can adjust the speed of double-clicking.

Using Windows

A window is an area of the screen that is assigned a specific purpose. There are two types of windows: application windows and document windows. *Application windows* contain running programs or applications such as Excel or Word for Windows. *Document windows* contain documents used with applications, such as a Word document or an Excel spreadsheet. An application window may contain one or more document windows. The Accessories and Main group windows that you have been looking at on your screen and in the figures are document windows; whereas the Program Manager window is an application window. An application window has a menu bar; a document window does not. Both types of windows have a title bar with the window title in the middle, the Control menu box on the left, and the minimize and maximize buttons on the right.

The Windows Environment

Windows can be quite small, they can fill the screen, or they can be any size in between. By clicking on the maximize button, you can make a window fill the screen. When you maximize a window, a new button—the *restore button*—appears in place of the maximize button. If you click on the restore button, the window is returned to the size it was just before you clicked on the maximize button. As you have already seen, if you click on the minimize button, the window shrinks to an icon at the bottom of the window or screen. Then by double-clicking on that icon you can return it to an open window that is the size it was when you minimized it.

You can make an open window that is not maximized any size by dragging on the border of the window. When you place the mouse pointer on the border around the window, the mouse pointer becomes a double-headed arrow. By pressing the mouse button while you see the double-headed arrow and dragging the border, you can change the window size. By dragging on any side, you can change the size of the window in one dimension. By dragging on a corner, you can change the size in two dimensions—for example, you can enlarge a window upward and to the right by dragging the top-right corner.

Finally, both an open application window and an application icon can be dragged anywhere on the screen. A document window can be dragged only within its application window. To drag an open window, point on the title bar of the window (anywhere except on the Control menu box or the minimize or maximize buttons) and drag it where you want. To drag an icon, point anywhere on the icon and drag it.

Practice using some of the window-sizing features with these instructions:

1. Click on the maximize button in the upper-right corner of the Accessories window. The Accessories window expands to fill the Program Manager window, as you can see in Figure 2-5.

   Notice that the title bar has changed. The title is now "Program Manager - [Accessories]," which tells you that the Accessories window has filled the Program Manager window. Also note that the Control menu box in the title bar is for the Program Manager, while the Control menu box in the menu bar is for the Accessories window.

Networking Windows for Workgroups

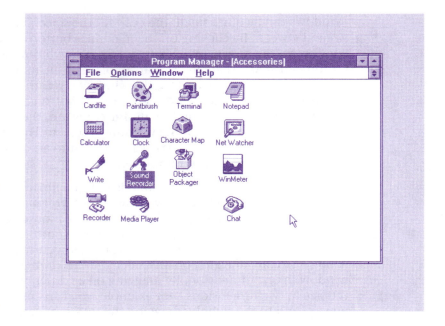

Accessories group window maximized within the Program Manager
Figure 2-5.

2. Click on the restore button that now appears just under the Program Manager's maximize button. The Accessories window returns to its former size.

3. Click on the maximize button of the Program Manager window. The window expands to fill the screen.

4. Click on the restore button of the Program Manager window, and the window shrinks to its former size.

5. Point on the lower-right corner border of the Accessories window. A diagonal double-headed arrow appears if you are precisely on the border.

6. Drag the lower-right corner toward the bottom right until the Accessories window is as big as you can make it.

7. Drag the lower-right corner toward the upper left until the Accessories window is about one-quarter of the size it was before you enlarged it, as shown in Figure 2-6.

8. Point on the title bar of the Accessories menu—anywhere but the Control menu box and the minimize and maximize buttons.

The Windows Environment

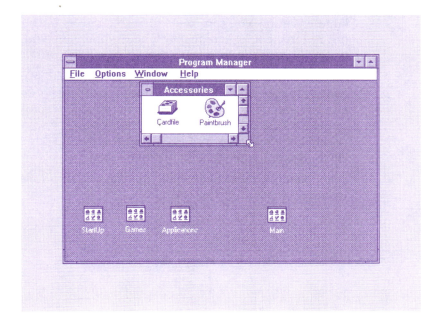

Shrunken Accessories group window
Figure 2-6.

9. Drag the Accessories window to the lower-right corner of the Program Manager window. Notice that you cannot get out of the Program Manager window.
10. By pointing on the Program Manager's title bar, drag it around the screen.
11. Click on the minimize button of the Program Manager window. It closes to an icon at the bottom of the screen.
12. Double-click on the Program Manager icon. Notice how the Program Manager and Accessories windows open in the same location in which they closed.
13. Drag both the Accessories window and the Program Manager window back to their original positions, as shown in Figure 2-6.

Using Scroll Bars

A window on the screen is just that—an opening through which you can see something displayed. If what is displayed is very small, a small window adequately displays it all. If what is displayed is very large, the largest window you can create (one that covers the entire screen) may not be large enough to display it all. In that case, you can horizontally or vertically move, or scroll, what the window contains.

Imagine that you are looking through a microscope at a glass slide containing a specimen. You must move the slide both up and down and left and right to see all of the specimen. The scroll bars perform the same function for the contents of a window. The *scroll bars* move the *contents of the window* (not the window itself) up or down (that is, vertically) or left or right (horizontally).

Each of the two scroll bars has three mechanisms for moving the window contents, as shown here:

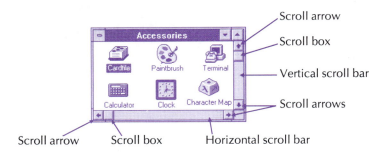

First, there are four *scroll arrows,* one at each end of each scroll bar. By clicking on one of the scroll arrows, you can move the contents in the direction of the arrow by a small increment—for example, one line vertically. Second, there are the two square *scroll boxes* in the scroll bars. By dragging a scroll box, you can move the window contents by a corresponding proportional amount. Third, there are the scroll bars themselves. By clicking on the scroll bars (in areas other than the scroll arrows and scroll boxes), you can move the window contents by the height or width of one window in the direction corresponding to where you clicked.

Use the reduced Accessories window and the following instructions to try out the scroll bars:

1. Click on the down scroll arrow at the bottom of the vertical scroll bar. Notice that the window contents move up and you see

The Windows Environment

information below what was previously shown. Notice also that the scroll box has moved down in the scroll bar.

The position of the scroll box in the scroll bar represents the approximate position of the portion of the file displayed within the total file. When the vertical scroll box is at the top of its scroll bar, you are looking at the top of the file. When the horizontal scroll bar is at the left end of its scroll bar, you are looking at the left edge of the file. When both scroll boxes are in the middle of their scroll bars, you are looking at the middle of the file.

2. Click on the right scroll arrow several times until the scroll box is at the far right of the horizontal scroll bar.

3. Click on the horizontal scroll bar, on the left of the scroll box, until the scroll box is at the far left of the scroll bar. Notice how it takes fewer clicks to move over the length of the scroll bar.

4. Drag the vertical scroll box a small amount toward the middle of the scroll bar. Note how this allows you to move the display area in very precise increments.

The three scrolling mechanisms give you three levels of control. Clicking on the scroll bar moves the display area the farthest, dragging the scroll box can move the display area in the smallest and most precise increments, and clicking on the scroll arrows moves the display area a small to intermediate amount.

Now that you can scroll the Accessories window, your next step is to use it to select an application.

Starting Applications

The Accessories window contains the icons for the various accessories available in Windows. Each of these accessories is an application that runs under Windows. To start an application you simply double-click on its icon. Do that now to work with several application windows.

1. Scroll the Accessories window until you can see the Clock icon.

2. Double-click on the Clock icon. The Clock application starts and opens a window entitled "Clock," as shown in Figure 2-7. (If your clock is in digital mode it will display the date and seconds.)

Networking Windows for Workgroups

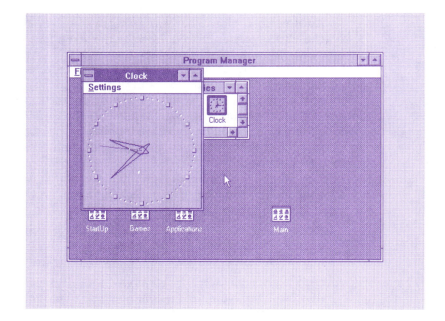

Clock window open
Figure 2-7.

Notice how the Clock window's title bar and border are dark with light letters while the Program Manager's title bar and border have become light with dark letters. This means that the Clock is now the active application and the Program Manager is inactive.

NOTE: There may be some differences between your screen and the figures and illustrations shown in this book. That is due to the differences in displays, display adapters, and in the options you selected during Windows installation.

3. Click on the Clock's maximize button. The Clock window expands to fill the screen.

4. Click on the restore button and the Clock window returns to its original size.

5. Drag the Clock window (by dragging on the Clock window's title bar anywhere except the buttons or the Control menu box) to the lower-right corner of the screen.

The Windows Environment

6. Click on the Accessories window to activate the Program Manager, scroll the Accessories window until you can see the Notepad icon, and then double-click on it. The Notepad application starts; its window opens and becomes the active window, as shown in Figure 2-8.
7. Drag the Notepad window until it overlaps but does not completely cover the Clock (unless it was that way originally).
8. Click on the Clock to activate it. Notice how it now overlaps the Notepad.
9. Click on the Notepad window to reactivate it, and then drag on the upper-left corner to reduce the size of the Notepad to about half its original size so you can see the Accessories window.
10. Click on the Accessories window to activate the Program Manager, scroll the Accessories window until you can see the Paintbrush icon, and then double-click on it. The Paintbrush application starts; its window opens and becomes the active window.
11. Size the Paintbrush window so you can see parts of the Clock, the Notepad, and the Program Manager windows, as shown in Figure 2-9.

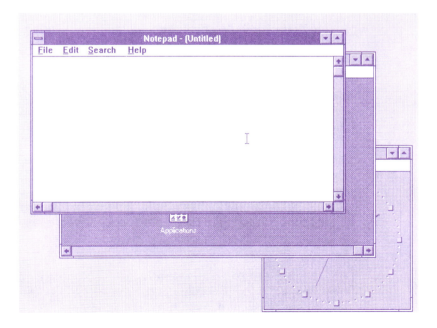

Notepad window open
Figure 2-8.

36

Networking Windows for Workgroups

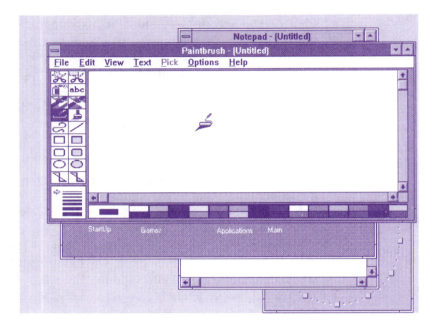

Paintbrush window added
Figure 2-9.

You now have four applications running in Windows: the Program Manager, the Clock, the Notepad, and Paintbrush. Move them around, size them in various ways, and activate first one and then another. Continue this until you are comfortable working with these windows.

Notice that as you move the mouse among these windows the mouse pointer changes. In the Paintbrush window the mouse pointer can be a paint roller, a dot, a cross hairs, or several other shapes. In the Notepad window the pointer is an I-beam. In the Clock and Program Manager windows the pointer is the familiar arrow. The pointer is telling you what can be done when it is in the various windows. In Paintbrush you can draw with the dot and use the cross hairs for cutting away a part of a drawing. The I-beam is used with text; its skinny nature allows you to insert it between characters. When you click an I-beam you are establishing an *insertion point,* which determines where text you type is placed.

12. Click on the minimize button of the Notepad, Clock, Paintbrush, and Accessories windows. The first three become application icons at the bottom of the screen while the Accessories window becomes

The Windows Environment

the now familiar group icon at the bottom of the Program Manager window, as shown in Figure 2-10.

Notice how the clock still tells time even though it has turned into an icon. This is generally true about application icons—they are running programs that are just temporarily inactive. The only differences between an inactive window and an application icon are the amount of the screen they use and how you activate them. You must double-click on an icon to activate it while you need only click once on an inactive window.

13. Drag the three application icons to reorder them, and place them in other locations on the screen just to see how you can do it. When you are finished, drag them back to their original location and order, as shown in Figure 2-10.

Manipulating windows and their icons—by selecting, dragging, maximizing, minimizing, sizing, and scrolling—are basic skills in the Windows environment. Practice these techniques until they are second nature. You will use them often. Another primary skill in the Windows environment is the use of menus.

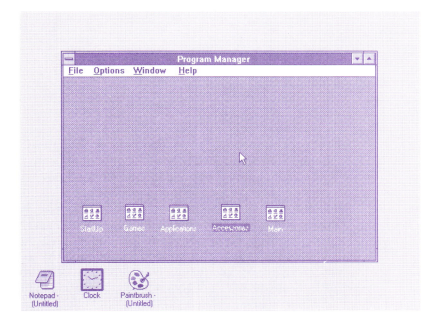

Applications windows turned into icons
Figure 2-10.

Using Menus

You use menus to give instructions to Windows and its applications. MS-DOS, by itself, is command-oriented—you type commands at a system prompt. Within Windows, you give a command by making a choice on a menu. The menus available to you at any given time are shown in the menu bar. By clicking on a menu name—*selecting* a menu—you open the menu. By clicking on a menu option—*choosing* an option—you make the option perform its function.

Menu options can represent several different functions. Often when you choose a menu option you are telling the application to carry out a command, such as saving a file or copying something. Other menu options allow you to set parameters or defaults for the items you are working on, like selecting the size of a page to be printed or the color of an object. Still other menu options are themselves menus—in other words, selecting a menu option opens another menu. This is called *cascading menus*.

Look at several menus now and get a feel for how they operate.

1. Click on the Program Manager's File menu. It opens as shown here:

The Program Manager's File menu has eight options. Notice that two of the options (Move and Copy) are dimmed while others are not. Options are dimmed to indicate that they are not available in the context of what you are doing. For example, if you do not have a selected object in the current window's workspace, you cannot move an object in that window; therefore, the Move option is dim. Many of the options, such as New, Copy, and Run, have an ellipsis (. . .) after them. When you select such an option, a dialog box opens. A *dialog box* is a place for you to provide further information or answer questions about the option you selected. For example, if you ask to save a file but you

The Windows Environment

have not yet provided the application with a filename, a dialog box opens asking you for the filename.

2. Click on New in the File menu.

   A dialog box opens asking if you want to add a new group or a new program to a group, and what to name the group or application.

3. Click on Cancel to close the dialog box.

4. Click on the File menu again. Then click on Properties and Run to look at their dialog boxes. Click on Cancel to close the dialog boxes.

5. Click on the Options, Window, and Help menus in succession, to look at each of them.

Notice in the Window menu that one of the listed windows has a check mark to the left of it. This means that window is currently active. One of the options of the Window menu allows you to choose the active window. When you click on your choice, a check mark is placed beside it so that the next time you open the menu you can tell which is active.

Notice also that a menu option may have a keystroke or series of keystrokes to the right of the option name. These are *shortcut keys*; for example, in the File menu, F7 is opposite the Move option. By pressing this key you can choose the menu option directly without first opening the menu.

Using Dialog Boxes

As you have seen, dialog boxes are a means of providing information about an option you have chosen. The dialog boxes you just looked at are rather simple, with only a couple of items. Dialog boxes can be very complex, with many different components. Windows uses several types of components to gather different types of information. These components are shown in the dialog boxes displayed in Figures 2-11 and 2-12. These Word for Windows and Excel dialog boxes are used for opening files and setting up a page to be printed, respectively.

Following is a description of the various dialog box components and their uses.

Networking Windows for Workgroups

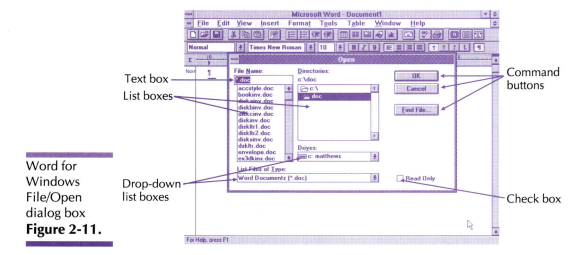

Word for Windows File/Open dialog box
Figure 2-11.

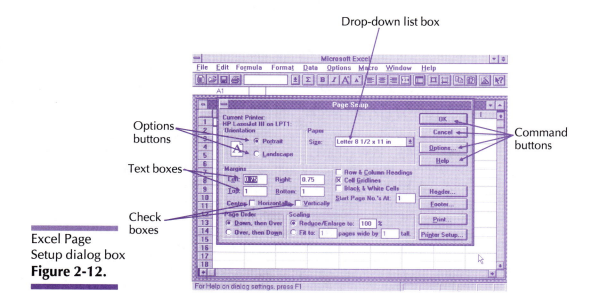

Excel Page Setup dialog box
Figure 2-12.

The Windows Environment

- ✦ **Check box**   Select several items from among a series of options by clicking on as many check boxes as desired to select those options. When selected, a check box contains an X; otherwise, the box is empty.

- ✦ **Command button**   Take immediate action by clicking on a command button. For example, close a dialog box, cancel a command, open another dialog box, or expand the current dialog box. The most common command button, OK, is used to close a dialog box. An ellipsis (...) indicates that a command button opens another dialog box, and two greater-than symbols (>>) indicate that a command button expands the current dialog box.

- ✦ **Drop-down list box**   Use a drop-down list box to select usually one item from a list in a constrained space. The current selection is shown, and clicking on the arrow to the right opens the drop-down list box. Click on the option desired, possibly using the scroll bar first.

- ✦ **List box**   Use a list box to select usually one item from a list. The current selection is highlighted. Click on the option desired, possibly using the scroll bar first.

- ✦ **Option button**   Click on an option button to select one item from a set of mutually exclusive options. A selection is changed by clicking on another option.

- ✦ **Text box**   Use a text box to enter text, such as a filename. The mouse pointer turns into an I-beam in a text box. Clicking the mouse in a text box places an insertion point, and any text typed will go to the left of the insertion point. If you don't click your mouse to place an insertion point, any selected text in a text box is replaced by anything typed. The Del key removes existing selected text in a text box.

Dialog boxes provide a very powerful and fast means of communicating with Windows and its applications. It is important that you know these terms and are comfortable using dialog boxes.

Using the Keyboard

You can do almost everything (except enter text) with a mouse, but in several instances the keyboard provides a useful shortcut. You have seen how several of the menu options have direct shortcut keys. You can also choose any of the other menu options with a general keyboard procedure. You can open any menu by pressing [Alt] (you do not have to hold it down) followed by the underlined letter in the menu name. After pressing [Alt] you can also use [←] and [→] to highlight a menu name, and then [↓] to open the menu and highlight an option. After a menu is open you can choose an option by typing the underlined letter in the option name or highlighting the option with the arrow keys and pressing [Enter]. You can also press [Enter] to open a menu once you have highlighted the menu name, and the [F10] function key can be used in place of [Alt] to initiate the process. To cancel a menu selection and return to the workspace, press [Alt] or [F10] a second time. To cancel a menu selection but stay in the menu bar so that another menu selection can be made, press [Esc].

Give the mouse a rest for a moment and access several menu options using the keyboard.

1. Press [Alt]-[F] to open the Program Manager's File menu.

2. Type **R** to select the Run option. The Run dialog box opens.

3. Press [Tab] to move among the various fields in the dialog box and then press [Esc] to cancel the dialog box, close the File menu, and deactivate the menu bar.

In general, to move around in a dialog box you first press [Tab] to move through the major groups of options, normally from left to right and top to bottom, or use [Shift]-[Tab] to reverse the direction. Alternatively, press and hold [Alt] while typing the underlined letter in the option or group name to move directly to that option or group. Then use the arrow keys to highlight an option within a group and use [Spacebar] to make the final selection of the option. Finally, press [Enter] to complete and close the dialog box.

4. Press [F10] to reactivate the menu bar.

5. Press [→] twice to move to the Window menu.

6. Press [Enter] to open the Window menu, then press [↓] four times to highlight the second group window name.

7. Press [Enter] to select the highlighted menu item and open the selected group window.

8. Press [Alt]-[-] (hyphen) to open the Control menu of the open group window and then type **N** to minimize it once again to an icon.

The Windows Environment

Using the Control Menu

The Control menu, located in the upper-left corner of most windows and dialog boxes, allows you to perform many other Windows functions with the keyboard that you have previously learned to perform with the mouse. There is some difference among Control menus but, for the most part, the options are the same.

Click on the Control menu box or press [Alt]-[Spacebar] to open the Program Manager's Control menu shown here:

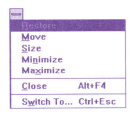

The options available in this Control menu and their functions are as follows:

Option	Function
Restore	Restores the window to the size it was prior to being minimized or maximized
Move	Allows moving the window with the keyboard
Size	Allows sizing the window with the keyboard
Minimize	Minimizes the window size to an icon
Maximize	Maximizes the window size—normally, to fill the screen
Close	Closes the window
Switch To	Switches among the currently running applications and allows rearrangement of their icons and windows

The following additional options are available on other Control menus:

Option	Function	
Edit	Opens an Edit menu with four options (non-Windows applications in 386 enhanced mode only):	
	Mark	Allows selection of text to be copied to the Clipboard
	Copy	Copies text to the Clipboard
	Paste	Copies the contents of the Clipboard to the insertion point in the active document window
	Scroll	Scrolls the active document window
Next	Switches to the next open document window or document icon (on document windows only)	
Paste	Copies the contents of the Clipboard to the insertion point in the active document window (real and standard mode only)	
Settings	Allows entering settings for multitasking (non-Windows applications in 386 enhanced mode only)	

With the Control menu open, try several of its options using the keyboard.

1. Press ⬇ to highlight Move and press [Enter] to choose it. The pointer becomes a four-headed arrow.

2. Press one or more of the arrow keys to move the window in the direction you choose. An outline of the window shows you where you are going.

3. When the outline of the window is where you want it, press [Enter]. If you want to cancel the move, press [Esc] instead of pressing [Enter].

4. Press [Alt]-[Spacebar] to reopen the Program Manager's (the active window) Control menu.

5. Press ⬇ twice to highlight Size and press [Enter] to choose it. The pointer becomes a four-headed arrow.

The Windows Environment

6. Press one arrow key to select one side whose size you want to change, or press two arrow keys simultaneously to select two sides whose sizes you want to change. (Pressing two arrow keys simultaneously is the same as selecting a corner with the mouse.)

7. Press one or two arrows until the window is the size you want it. Then press `Enter`. If you want to cancel the sizing, press `Esc` instead of pressing `Enter`.

8. Press `Alt`-`Spacebar` to reopen the Program Manager's Control menu.

9. Type **X** to choose Maximize. The Program Manager window expands to fill the screen.

10. Press `Alt`-`Spacebar` to open the Program Manager's Control menu and press `Enter` to choose Restore. The Program Manager window returns to its original size.

11. Press `Alt`-`Spacebar` again and type **N** to choose Minimize. The Program Manager window shrinks to an icon.

12. Press `Alt`-`Esc` to cycle through the various application icons (or windows if any are open). When you have reached the Program Manager again, press `Alt`-`Spacebar` to open the Control menu.

13. Press `Enter` to choose Restore. The Program Manager window reopens at its last size and location.

14. Press `Ctrl`-`F6` or `Ctrl`-`Tab` to cycle through the various document (group) icons (or windows if any are open).

15. When you reach Main, press `Alt`-`-` (hyphen) to open the Main group's Control menu.

16. Choose Restore by pressing `Enter`, since Restore is already highlighted. Your screen should look like that shown in Figure 2-13.

Notice that for application windows and document windows you use different key combinations to open their Control menus and to cycle through windows and icons. Use `Alt`-`Spacebar` to open an application window Control menu, and use `Alt`-`Esc` to cycle through the application windows and icons that are running (on the screen). Use `Alt`-`-` (hyphen) to open a document window Control menu, and use `Ctrl`-`F6` or `Ctrl`-`Tab` to cycle through the document windows and icons in the active application window.

One important Control menu option you have not tried yet is Close. In most windows, Close simply closes the window. In the Program

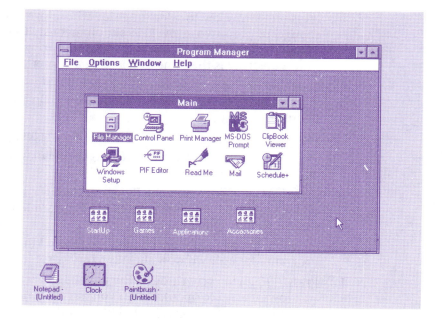

Main group displayed in the Program Manager window
Figure 2-13.

Manager, it closes Windows and returns you to DOS. You will do that later in the chapter. Once the Control menu is open, you can choose Close in the normal ways: by clicking on it, by highlighting it and pressing (Enter), or by typing **C**. You can choose Close with the Control menu closed by double-clicking on the Control menu box or by pressing (Alt)-(F4).

The keyboard and the Control menu are important adjuncts to the mouse. But they should be viewed as that and not the other way around. With Windows the mouse is by far the most effective and expeditious way to do things. For that reason, this book usually has instructions for the mouse. Keyboard instructions are given only for shortcut keys when you are already typing on the keyboard.

Using the Main Group Applications

The Main group, which should currently be displayed on your screen, includes ten applications that have the following functions:

The Windows Environment

Application	Function
File Manager	View and manipulate files and manage disks.
Control Panel	Set defaults such as color, double-click speed, and date and time.
Print Manager	Manage queuing and printing of files.
MS-DOS Prompt	Provide a DOS command-line prompt at which any DOS command can be entered. Type **exit** to return to Windows.
ClipBook Viewer	Display the contents of both the Clipboard and local and remote ClipBooks.
Windows Setup	Make changes to the hardware and software configuration you are using with Windows.
PIF Editor	Edit program information files (PIF) used to start non-Windows applications in Windows.
Read Me	Display notes on Windows for Workgroups that supplement the written documentation.
Mail	Send and receive electronic mail over a Windows for Workgroups network.
Schedule	Jointly track appointments and meetings of all members of a workgroup using a network and Windows for Workgroups.

Mail and Schedule will be discussed in depth in their own chapters—Chapters 7 and 8. Also, the Print Manager is discussed in Chapter 5 under "Using the Print Manager to Share a Printer." For now, take a brief look at the Control Panel, File Manager, and ClipBook viewer.

Setting Defaults with the Control Panel

The Control Panel is the primary place in Windows where you set the parameters or defaults that tell Windows how you want a number of different functions handled. Double-click on the Control Panel icon. The Control Panel opens as shown here:

Networking Windows for Workgroups

The Control Panel consists of the following functions, each with its own icon, for which you can set defaults.

✦ **Color** Set colors associated with the various parts of the screen.

✦ **Fonts** Set fonts available for both screen and printer(s).

✦ **Ports** Set communications parameters used with serial ports.

✦ **Mouse** Set behavior of the mouse, including the double-click rate, the speed the pointer moves across the screen, and whether the left or right mouse button is primary.

✦ **Desktop** Set characteristics of the screen or desktop, including the cursor blink rate, the presence or absence of a "magnetic" grid to better align objects, and the patterns used for various areas.

✦ **Keyboard** Set keyboard delay before repeating a key, and the repeat rate.

✦ **Printers** Set parameters applicable to your printer(s), including ports assigned, paper size and orientation, graphics resolution, and the identification of the default printer.

✦ **International** Set formats for numbers, currency, dates, and times.

✦ **Date/Time** Set the system date and time.

✦ **Network** Set parameters applicable to your network (available only if you are using a network).

✦ **386 Enhanced** Set sharing of peripheral devices and system resources in multitasking environment (available only if you are using 386 enhanced mode).

The Windows Environment

◆ **Sound** Set presence or absence of the warning sound or beep and, if you have a sound board, the sound to use for various functions.

◆ **Drivers** Set addition, removal, and configuration of drivers for audio and video equipment.

You can set any of the functions by selecting the appropriate icon (by clicking on it) and then entering the necessary parameters in the dialog box that opens. Try that now by setting the double-click rate of the mouse.

1. Double-click on the Mouse icon in the Control Panel. The Mouse dialog box opens as shown here:

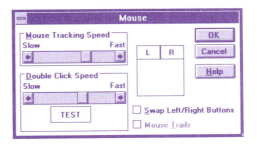

2. If you are left-handed, or for any reason want to make the right mouse button the primary mouse button, click on the Swap Left/Right Buttons check box at the bottom middle of the screen. You have to start using the other mouse button immediately.

3. Double-click on the Test command button. If the button darkens, the double-click speed is set properly for you. If the Test button does not darken, you are double-clicking either too fast or too slow and you need to change the speed with the next step.

4. Click on the Slow or Fast scroll arrow and try double-clicking again.

5. Repeat steps 3 and 4 until the double-clicking speed is set correctly and the Test command button darkens.

6. When you are done with the mouse settings, click OK to close the dialog box and return to the Control Panel window.

   You will find many similar controls in other control panels. Chapter 4 will discuss the Networking control panel. On your own, look at the other control panels. You'll find you can do a lot to tailor Windows to your tastes. Unless you want to change something, click on Cancel in each dialog box so you don't change anything inadvertently.

7. When you are done with the Control Panel, double-click on the Control menu box in the upper-left corner. This closes the Control Panel and returns you to the Main group window of the Program Manager.

Using the File Manager

The File Manager provides all of the customary DOS file-handling commands, such as COPY, DELETE, and RENAME, as well as a number of file-manipulation tools that up to now have only been available with such packages as XTree and PC Tools. Open the File Manager now and look at some of its facilities.

Double-click on the File Manager icon in the Main group window of the Program Manager. The File Manager window opens, and a directory window for your root directory also opens, as shown in Figure 2-14.

The directory tree provides a very powerful way of viewing and working with your directories and their files. The initial view shows you an alphabetical list of all the subdirectories under your root directory in a "tree" window on the left, and a directory of all contents (both subdirectories and files) within the root directory on the right. Each subdirectory is represented by a file folder. Files are represented either by a single sheet with a folded corner (data files) or by a miniature window (.COM, .EXE, and other executable files). You can choose different ways to display your directories and files. For example, you can display either the tree, or the directory, or both; and you can use indicators to show whether a file folder contains subdirectories. You may open and list the files and subdirectories in any directory by double-clicking on the folder icon.

In the directory window you can select or highlight files you want to move, copy, rename, or delete. To move a file, drag its icon from the current directory on the right to a new directory or subdirectory in the tree window on the left. To copy a file, press and hold Ctrl while you drag the file icon. If you wish to move, copy, rename, or delete several files at one time and the files are listed sequentially, click on the first

The Windows Environment

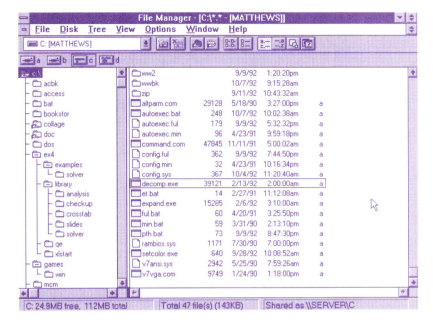

Figure 2-14.
File Manager displaying the root directory

filename, and then press and hold (Shift) while you click on the last filename in the sequence. If you want to select several files that are not in sequence, press and hold (Ctrl) while you click on each of the items. To cancel a selected item, press and hold (Ctrl) while you click on the item. To delete or rename files, select the files and then choose the appropriate command from the File menu.

The File menu provides access to several other file functions, as you can see here:

Among the File menu options is creating a directory. Use that command now to create a directory named DATA.

1. Click on the File Manager's File menu to open it.
2. Click on Create Directory to choose that option. The Create Directory dialog box opens, as shown here:

If you previously selected the directory under which you wish to create a new subdirectory, all you need to enter is the new directory's name. Otherwise you need to type the full *pathname* of the new directory, which would include the drive and directory name.

3. Type **data** or, if necessary, precede it with the pathname you want to use; for example, type **c:\data**.
4. Press [Enter] to close the dialog box, create the directory, and return to the File Manager window.
5. When you are done with the File Manager, double-click on its Control menu box to close it and return to the Main group window of the Program Manager.

Using the ClipBook Viewer

With the release of Windows for Workgroups, the Clipboard Viewer has been replaced with the ClipBook Viewer. The *ClipBook Viewer* lets you view the Clipboard as well as permanently store the Clipboard contents on one of many pages in the ClipBook. When you have stored something in the ClipBook, you can turn off your computer and then come back, turn it on again, and find the information you placed in the ClipBook. With the Clipboard, you lose its contents when you leave Windows. Equally important, items in the ClipBook can be shared with other members connected to a network. Sharing a ClipBook on a network will be discussed in Chapters 5 and 6.

The Windows Environment

Try putting information in the ClipBook and taking it out again with the following exercise:

1. To create some information to store, double-click on the Notepad to open it. (If the Notepad is not visible on your screen, open your Accessories group by double-clicking on it, use your scroll bars to display the Notepad, and then double-click on the Notepad.)
2. Type your name or anything else—for example, **Now is the time.** Press and hold [Shift] while pressing [Home] to highlight what you just typed, and then press the shortcut keys, [Ctrl]-[C], to copy what you typed into the Clipboard.
3. Double-click on the Notepad's Control menu box to close the Notepad. Answer No, you don't want to save what you just typed, and then double-click on the ClipBook Viewer to open it as you see here:

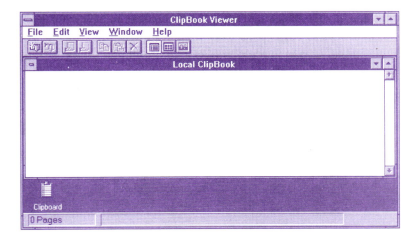

4. Double-click on the Clipboard to open it and confirm that the text you copied to it is there (if it isn't, you need to repeat steps 1 through 3). Once you have confirmed it is there, click on the Clipboard's minimize button to return it to an icon.
5. Click on the Edit menu and then click on Paste to paste the contents of the Clipboard into the ClipBook. (You can also use the shortcut keys, [Ctrl]-[V].) The Paste dialog box opens asking you to fill

Networking Windows for Workgroups

in the Page Name where you want to store the current Clipboard entry, as shown here:

NOTE: "Page Name" is really a misnomer. Because you can only store one thing on each "page," it should probably be called "item name." In any case, you can think of it that way.

Notice also, the check box that allows you to determine if you want to share this item with others on the network. If you check it, anyone on the network will be able to copy the item. If you don't check it, only you will be able to access the item.

6. Type **Item 1**, click on Share Item Now, and on OK. A second dialog box will open giving you several choices on sharing the item. These will be discussed further in Chapter 5. For now, click on OK and the item will go into the ClipBook. An icon with the name and a hand holding a notebook appears. The hand indicates that the item is shared.

7. Double-click on the icon, and it opens to show the information you originally placed on the Clipboard. This is called Full Page view. To return to the icon view, select the View menu and choose Table of Contents.

NOTE: When you open the View menu, you will notice that there is a third view called Thumbnails, which shows you a very small view of the item—it's so small you can just barely read it.

The Windows Environment

8. Double-click on the ClipBook's Control menu box to close the ClipBook.

At this moment, the information you placed on the Clipboard is still there. As soon as you place something else there, the original information is erased. When that happens, you can restore that information from the ClipBook by selecting the item and choosing Copy from the Edit menu or pressing `Ctrl`-`C`. You can then paste the item onto any other document.

The ClipBook provides handy permanent (until you erase it) storage for Clipboard items that you can share over a network. As such, it is a worthwhile addition to Windows.

Getting Help

Online help in Windows is very extensive, and it can be context-sensitive—providing specific help about what you are doing. You can get help by several methods. The fastest method is to press `F1`. You'll get a table of contents of Help topics. In most Windows applications, you can also press `Shift`-`F1`. The mouse pointer will become a question mark that you can click on something—a menu option for example—to get specific help about that option. The second method of getting help is to click on the Help button available in most dialog boxes. The final and most general-purpose method of getting help is to use the Help menu on most application windows. You can access the Help menu by either clicking on it or pressing `Alt`-`H`.

To look at the Program Manager's Help facility, click on Help in the menu bar. The Program Manager's Help menu opens, as shown here:

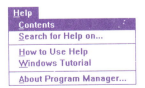

Most Help menus within Windows have the same set of options. These options, with the information they provide, are as follows:

Networking Windows for Workgroups

Option	Information Provided
Contents	Topic summary
Search for Help on	Quick access to Help topics
How to Use Help	Tutorial on how to use Help
Windows Tutorial	Starts the Windows tutorial (Program Manager only)
About	Information about the application and your system resources

With the Help menu open, you can get information about the File menu commands, for example, with the following steps.

1. Click on Contents. A window appears, as shown in Figure 2-15. In the Help window you make a choice by clicking on an underlined topic. When the pointer is pointing on a topic that can be chosen, it becomes a pointing hand, as shown in Figure 2-15.
2. Click on File Menu Commands. The File Menu Commands Help window opens.

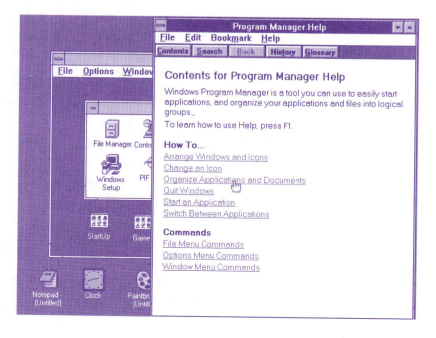

Program Manager initial Help window
Figure 2-15.

The Windows Environment

The command buttons at the top of a Help window return you to Contents (Contents), allow you to search for a topic (Search), retrace the path you have taken to get to the current Help window (Back), show you a listing of your previous Help choices (History), or show topics covered in alphabetical order (Glossary).

3. Use the Help command buttons on your own to review the Windows Help facility.

4. When you are finished reviewing Help, double-click on the Control menu box to close it. You will be returned to the Main group window of the Program Manager.

Leaving Windows

Windows and many of the applications that run under Windows use temporary files to store intermediate information as the program is running. If you leave the applications and Windows in the correct manner, these temporary files are automatically erased, and you are reminded to save any files you have not saved. The correct way to leave any window is to double-click on its Control menu box or press Alt-F4. Simply do this until you reach the DOS prompt, and you have correctly left Windows. Then, and only then, can you safely turn off your computer.

Arrange your Program Manager window the way you want it to be when you next use Windows and then leave Windows with these steps:

1. Using the techniques you learned in this chapter, size and position your windows and icons the way you want for ongoing use of Windows.

2. Double-click on the Program Manager's Control menu box. You are asked to confirm that you want to leave Windows. Click on OK to leave Windows. You are returned to the DOS prompt.

This chapter has laid a foundation on which you can begin to add specific knowledge of networking. Windows is not a simple subject, but it provides a very powerful framework that is greatly enhanced by networking. You now have enough knowledge of that framework to set up your network, which you will do in Chapter 3.

CHAPTER

3

SELECTING AND INSTALLING NETWORK HARDWARE

Your Windows for Workgroups LAN consists of both the Windows for Workgroups network software and the network hardware that provides the electrical signals and the physical connections between the computers on your LAN. This chapter deals with the hardware part of your LAN. In it you learn how to plan for your LAN, choose the type of network interface card and topology to use for your LAN, how to configure and install the hardware, and how to troubleshoot problems. As you read this chapter, develop a written plan to make implementing the LAN as smooth and painless as possible for the members of your workgroup. Getting the hardware part of a LAN to work properly is usually much more difficult than getting the software to work.

Planning Your LAN

Even if your workgroup is small you should develop a plan for it. This plan can serve as a reference for troubleshooting or future expansion of the LAN, and will save you time in the long run. As you read the remaining sections in this chapter you will see why you need this information. Use the following steps to develop your plan.

1. Start a LAN notebook for recording this plan, and add notes to it as you make changes to your LAN.

2. For each computer that you want to include in your Windows for Workgroups LAN, record as much of the following information as possible:

✦ The make and model, processor type and speed, and amount of conventional, expanded, and extended memory (RAM) in the computer. Also record the brand of mouse (if any) attached, and the type and brand of monitor and video card.

✦ The type of unused slot(s) available on the system board. You will have to remove the cover to determine this. Also note whether there is an 8-bit card installed in a 16-bit slot (you will see how to tell the difference later in this chapter), and if so, whether there is an unused 8-bit slot that it could be moved to.

✦ The types of disk drives installed on the computer. For floppy drives, include the size (5.25-inch or 3.5-inch) and format (double- or high-density) and drive letter (A, B) of each. For hard drives list the size in megabytes (MB), the drive letter (C, D, E), and the CMOS type (17, 37, and so on) for each. The CMOS type can be ascertained by running the MSD.EXE program included with Windows (discussed later in this chapter), or by running the CMOS Setup program when booting the computer (consult your dealer if you don't know how to do this).

Selecting and Installing Network Hardware

◆ The types of cards plugged into slots on the system board. For each card that uses a hardware interrupt request line (IRQ) and I/O port address (for example, serial and parallel I/O cards, internal fax and modem cards, bus mouse cards, CD-ROM, and tape drives) try to determine the interrupt request line number and I/O port address used. Tables of interrupts and port addresses and the devices typically using them are included later in this chapter. Refer to the documentation that came with the computer and add-on cards for help with this.

◆ The location of the computer in relation to the others in the workgroup. Especially if your LAN will be larger than three or four nodes, prepare a drawing of your office floor plan that includes all the computers, printers, and other connected devices, and include measured or estimated distances between the computers. Also note the locations of large machines with motors, including air conditioners, and recessed fluorescent light fixtures if you think that the cable will have to run in the ceiling. These devices are potential sources of electromagnetic interference, and should not have the cables routed close to them.

◆ The computer's operating system name and version, the amount of free space on the hard disk drive, and the resources on the computer (such as a printer, modem, fax machine, software application, or data files) that you will most likely want to share with others in the workgroup.

3. After gathering the information about the computers in your workgroup, look at each machine to determine how suitable it is for running the graphics-intensive Windows for Workgroups operating system. Consider the following:

◆ **Processor** Although Windows for Workgroups will run on a 286 processor, many users will not be pleased with the speed at which their applications run. In addition, a 286 computer is not able to share its resources with others on a Windows for Workgroups LAN. If you decide to purchase a computer for your LAN, the minimum recommended machine is a 386SX running at 20 megahertz.

◆ **Memory** Computer memory (RAM) is classified as conventional, upper, or extended, as shown in Figure 3-1.

Networking Windows for Workgroups

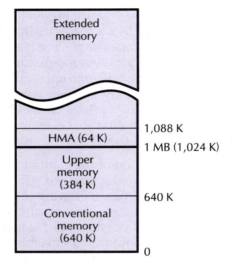

Types of memory in 286 and newer desktop computers
Figure 3-1.

The minimum amount of extended memory that a Windows for Workgroups LAN computer must have in order to share its resources is 3MB, but the more extended memory you add the better Windows will perform (up to about 16MB).

◆ **Hard drive** You will need at least 9.5MB of free space on each computer's hard disk (or 3.5MB if it already is running Windows 3.1) to install Windows for Workgroups. These minimums are sufficient only for a partial installation of the Windows for Workgroups software, and don't include space for any new Windows-based applications that you may want to add. Try to free up 15MB or more of hard disk space before installing Windows for Workgroups. If your hard disk drive controller is 100 percent compatible with the Western Digital WD1003 controller, Windows for Workgroups can use 32-bit disk access, which can speed up disk access and improve memory utilization when running in 386 enhanced mode.

◆ **Display** Windows for Workgroups is a very visual environment and makes heavy demands on the display adapter card. The more memory that the display adapter card has, the faster the screen will be updated. Particularly for graphical applications like

Selecting and Installing Network Hardware

computer-aided design (CAD), illustration, and desktop publishing software, replacing the standard display adapter with an *accelerator* (or coprocessor) card can dramatically improve the speed of displaying images. This is because these display adapter cards handle their own display data processing, rather than burdening the system CPU with this task. Try to provide each workgroup member with a VGA color display to help avoid eyestrain, and for the additional information that color provides.

4. Get the members of your workgroup together, discuss the tasks that are currently shared by members of the group, and brainstorm ideas for using the connectedness of the LAN to make these tasks easier or more effective. Find out who exchanges data on floppy disks. Identify the software applications used by workgroup members, and consider whether a LAN version that allows simultaneous updates of data would be helpful. Find out who will need individual training on Windows for Workgroups, and who is experienced enough to provide that training. Provide workgroup members with a summary of the meeting.

5. If printers are to be shared, decide who will be using them and what location would be the most convenient for the users when retrieving their printouts. Also consider the amount of disruption to the person using the connected computer when others retrieve their printouts. Locate the printer near the person who will refill it with paper and change ribbons or cartridges.

6. Decide which type of network interface card you will use for your network. Also consider the type of cabling that is most appropriate for your particular office layout and workgroup size. If your office is prewired with network cables, this might influence your choice of network cards. Work on the next step at the same time you work on this one.

7. Decide where your LAN cables will go. Refer to your office floor plan for this step, and verify that your drawing conforms to the physical reality of the planned routes. If your office is prewired with network cables in the walls, determine whether they are suitable for your LAN. Avoid running cables where people will walk on them or roll their chairs over them. Make sure to record in your LAN notebook the actual cable routes used.

Network Topologies

As you read in Chapter 1, the way in which the computers on your LAN are connected together is its topology. The two topologies typically used for small LANs are bus and star. Both Ethernet and ARCnet cards are available for either topology. Larger networks sometimes use a combination of these two topologies.

Bus Topology

Bus topology is simpler than star topology, and connecting it is straightforward. Cables are simply run from one computer to the next, until they are all connected into a long chain. The two ends of the bus (or trunk) must have special resistors called *terminators* attached.

Bus topology has some advantages over star topology: it uses less cable and is easier to install, since it can follow the easiest route as it snakes from one computer to another. With bus topology, adding a new computer without disrupting the rest of the LAN is easy.

A disadvantage of bus topology is that the single cable can become overloaded in heavy network traffic conditions. It is also more vulnerable to bad cable connections because a break anywhere in the cabling usually brings down the entire LAN and is typically hard to track down.

Star Topology

Star topology uses a central hub to which the individual nodes (computers) on the LAN are connected. Stars can be connected to each other to expand the network into a *tree,* which makes star topology flexible in the way it can be configured and expanded. Other advantages to star topology are easy diagnosis of cable problems and no bottleneck under heavy network traffic, because each node has its own cable to the central point. In addition, a bad cable brings down only the node to which the cable is connected, not the whole LAN.

Some drawbacks to the star configuration are that if the *hub* fails, the whole LAN goes down, and the hubs can be expensive. Also, more cable is required than for the bus scheme.

Selecting and Installing Network Hardware

Topology Summary

For the small Windows for Workgroups LAN with about five or fewer computers, a bus is usually the most appropriate topology. However, if you think that your LAN might expand later, start with the star topology, to give yourself some flexibility.

Star topology is more appropriate than bus topology for large LANs that connect multiple rooms or floors, or for flexibility in situations where the computers are moved frequently.

Network Cables

The two types of cable that you are likely to use in your Windows for Workgroups LAN are coaxial and twisted-pair. The network cards typically used in small LANs are available for either type of cable, so you can choose both the protocol and the topology that you want to use for your LAN.

Coaxial Cable

Coaxial cable (*coax*) consists of a central wire surrounded by a layer of insulation, a sleeve of braided wire surrounding that, and finally an insulating jacket that covers the braid. The types of coax used for networks looks like the type used for cable TV, but they have different electrical characteristics. Network coax cables have their type printed on the cable (for example, RG-58A/U for Ethernet and RG-62A/U for ARCnet), and it is important that you use the exact type that your network card is designed to use.

The thin coax cable typically used for small LANs has BNC ("twist-to-lock") connectors on the ends of the cables. These cables can be purchased complete with connectors, or you can construct your own. Be aware, however, that attaching the BNC connectors requires careful stripping of the coax insulation and precise crimping with an expensive special tool. If you plan to construct your own cables, purchase some extra connectors; you are likely to ruin a few while you learn the proper technique.

Figure 3-2 shows the components used to connect a computer when coaxial cable is used with bus topology. The connection at each network interface card consists of a *tee connector* fastened to the card, and the two cables attached to the tee connector. At each of the two end computers on the bus, a terminator is attached to the tee connector in place of the second cable.

When coaxial cable is used with the star topology, the cable is connected directly onto the network card, with no tee connector or terminator. The other end of the cable connects to a hub, and sometimes requires a terminator on unused connections. A hub simply provides a cross connection for the cables that plug into it. Hubs can be passive or active. *Active* hubs amplify the signals passing through them, allowing for longer cable lengths.

Twisted-Pair Cable

Twisted-pair cable consists of pairs of insulated wires twisted about each other, all enclosed in a jacket. You will find twisted-pair cable in some

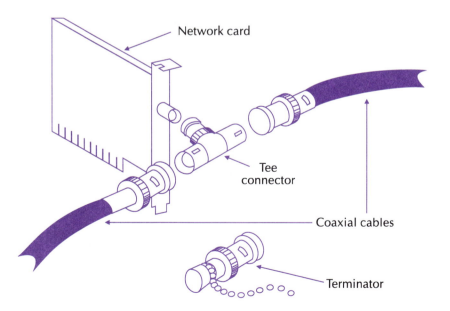

Components in a typical coaxial cable bus system
Figure 3-2.

Selecting and Installing Network Hardware

parts of telephone systems. This telephone cable is not necessarily appropriate for twisted-pair network cable, and might not be able to handle the higher rates of transmission used in LANs. Check the cable specifications of the network interface card you choose and compare them to any existing telephone cable in your building before deciding to use it.

The connectors used with twisted-pair cable are similar to the modular plugs used on most telephones, but they contain more contacts (typically six to eight). Instead of using tee connectors for bus networks, the cards have two sockets into which the two cables are plugged. Twisted-pair terminators are used at the ends of a bus, but are sometimes built into the network cards. Figure 3-3 shows the components in a typical twisted-pair bus system.

Twisted-pair cable is more susceptible to picking up interference from nearby large machinery, air conditioners, fluorescent light fixtures, and other devices that have strong magnetic fields. It must, therefore, be routed carefully to avoid these hazards, particularly on long runs. If your LAN is to be located in a magnetically "noisy" environment like a factory, use coaxial cable instead of twisted-pair (or use *shielded* twisted-pair).

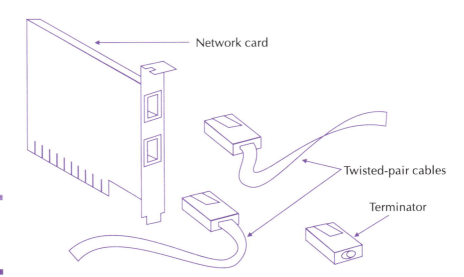

Twisted-pair bus system components
Figure 3-3.

The small diameter and flexibility of twisted-pair cable make it easier to run than coaxial, and it is less expensive per foot. The lower price for the cable is often offset by the need for an expensive hub, however, so find out exactly which components you will need for your particular workgroup layout before concluding that twisted-pair is cheaper than coaxial.

Network Interface Cards

Several different types of network cards exist, and they differ in the way they communicate (their *protocol*), the type of network topology they support, and the type of system expansion slot they are designed to fit. The primary functions of the network interface card are packaging the data into packets (similar to mail, where the message is enclosed in an envelope with the addresses on the outside), sending the packets out over the cables, intercepting packets addressed to the network interface card, and extracting messages from the received packets.

The two protocols that are most often used in small LANs like Windows for Workgroups are Ethernet and ARCnet. All the computers on your LAN typically use the same type of card. The Ethernet and ARCnet protocols are discussed after a brief explanation of system board expansion slots.

Expansion Slots

The network cards in your LAN must be designed for the type of system bus that each computer has. Most IBM-compatible computers use the ISA (Industry Standard Architecture) or EISA (Extended Industry Standard Architecture) type of bus; most IBM PS/2 computers use the MCA (Microchannel Architecture) type. (If you don't know which type of bus your computer has, consult the documentation that came with it, or ask your computer dealer.)

Network interface cards made for the ISA bus also fit EISA bus system boards, and are made in 8-bit and 16-bit versions (32-bit cards are also made for EISA bus systems on expensive super-fast servers). Figure 3-4 shows the two types of ISA system slots. The 8-bit ISA cards have a single set of edge connectors on them; 16-bit cards add a second set of connectors. The 16-bit cards are faster, more expensive, and cannot be used in 8-bit slots. The 8-bit cards can be used in either type of slot.

Selecting and Installing Network Hardware

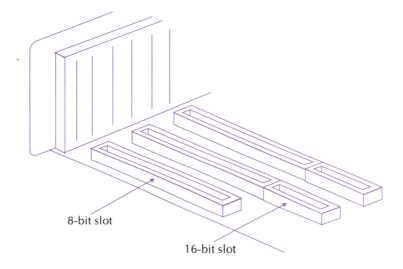

Figure 3-4.
ISA system board with 8-bit and 16-bit slots

Ethernet Cards

Ethernet cards are often chosen for small LANs. Although Ethernet cards are more expensive than ARCnet cards, they are two to three times faster than ARCnet. Ethernet cards are rated at 10 megabits (a megabit is about 1 million bits) per second transmission speed, but the actual rate at which messages travel is lower. An Ethernet LAN can even slow down to the speed of an ARCnet LAN when heavily loaded with network traffic.

Ethernet cards are made in 8- and 16-bit versions. They come in three types, based on the cable used: thick coaxial ("thicknet" or "10Base5"), thin coaxial ("thinnet," "cheapernet," or "10Base2"), and twisted-pair ("10Base-T"). Thick Ethernet cable is not often used for new installations due to its higher cost and more difficult installation. Thin Ethernet cable, RG-58A/U, is commonly used in small LANs because it is cheaper and easy to find.

Ethernet cards often use bus topology for connecting computers with coax, and star topology for connecting computers with twisted-pair cable (see "Network Topologies," earlier in this chapter for more information on these two topologies).

ARCnet Cards

The chief virtue of ARCnet cards is their low cost—about half the price of Ethernet cards. They are rated at 2.5 megabits per second, and are about one-third to one-half as fast as Ethernet cards. The speed of an ARCnet LAN is more constant under heavy load than an Ethernet LAN. Despite the slow speed of ARCnet, it might be an appropriate choice in some circumstances: if your LAN will never grow larger than four or five nodes, you need it mostly for sharing a printer, and cost is a significant factor, ARCnet might work well for you. Otherwise, for faster performance and future expansion options, Ethernet is a better investment for your small LAN.

ARCnet cards are available in both 8- and 16-bit versions, for either coaxial (RG-62A/U) or twisted-pair cable, and star or bus topology.

Network Card Settings

There are several settings that you probably have to make on your network interface cards; the documentation that comes with the network card specifies the settings required for your particular card. Whenever possible, use the default settings that the card comes with from the factory. These default settings are correct for many systems, but may not be correct for your system, depending on what other devices you have installed. Network cards usually have enough alternative settings to allow you to customize the card for your particular setup.

CAUTION: Before touching a computer card, be sure to discharge any static electricity from your body. The electronic components on the cards are easily damaged by static electricity, and you won't know that anything has happened until the board doesn't work. The metal back of a computer case that is plugged into a three-prong power outlet is a good ground, and simply touching it is sufficient to discharge the static electricity.

Selecting and Installing Network Hardware

Network interface cards usually have jumpers or switches for adjusting the settings, but some use a software utility (included with the card) to make changes. *Jumpers* are tiny plastic blocks that are pushed over pairs of pins to make an electrical connection. Shown here is a typical jumper block with the jumper placed on the center pair of pins (position 2 in this example):

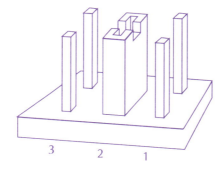

Switches on network cards (sometimes called DIP switches) consist of several miniature levers in a row, as shown here:

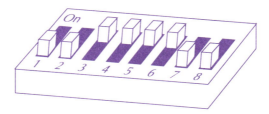

The individual switches can be moved into the desired on or off position using a tiny screwdriver or the tip of a pen (it is best not to use a pencil because of the possibility of graphite particles falling into the switch). The bank of switches must be configured to match exactly a chart or diagram shown in the card's documentation, and often sets an address that the card uses.

The settings that need to be set on most network interface cards are the interrupt request line, base I/O port address, base memory address, and node address. Each of these is discussed in the following sections.

Interrupt Request Line

The *interrupt request line* (IRQ) setting determines which hardware line the LAN card uses to "interrupt" the computer's processor and request attention to some processing task. If your network interface card contains this setting (most do), you must determine which IRQ numbers are being used by other cards in the computer, and adjust this setting on the network card to an unused IRQ number.

Table 3-1 lists all the IRQ numbers and the devices that typically use them. Your LAN plan should contain the IRQs used by all the devices in each computer; be sure to add them to the plan as you determine them.

Tip: Only 16-bit cards can use IRQ 9 and above. This alone may make it worthwhile using 16-bit cards.

IRQ 5 is often a good choice for the interrupt setting if you are using an 8-bit network interface card, since most computers do not use LPT2. Also, bus mice may use either IRQ 3 or 5, so you need to check which yours is using. For 16-bit cards, IRQ 10 or 11 are good choices.

Base I/O Port Address

The *base I/O port address* specifies the port address that the network card uses. This address is used by the computer's processor to communicate with the network interface card's *device driver* (the software that controls the card). Network cards use a series of addresses beginning with a *base* address, and are therefore usually expressed as a range of numbers in hexadecimal notation.

Selecting and Installing Network Hardware

IRQ	Device
0	Clock timer
1	Keyboard
2	Communications cards, EGA display adapters; also used to implement IRQ 9-15 on 80286 and newer computers
3	COM2 or COM4 serial ports
4	COM1 or COM3 serial ports
5	LPT2 parallel port or bus mouse
6	Floppy disk controller
7	LPT1 parallel port
8	Real-time clock
9	Usually available
10	Usually available
11	Usually available
12	Usually available
13	Math coprocessor
14	Hard disk controller
15	Usually available

Interrupt Request Line (IRQ) Numbers and the Devices That Typically Use Them
Table 3-1.

NOTE: The hexadecimal numbering system uses a base of 16 characters, in contrast to the usual numbering system that uses 10 characters (0 through 9). In order to get an extra 6 characters, the hexadecimal system uses the characters A through F, in addition to 0 through 9. When you count up in hexadecimal, the number after 9 is A, so counting from 0 to 15 would be 0, 1, 2, 3, 4, 5, 6, 7, 8, 9, A, B, C, D, E, F.

If your network card has a base I/O port address setting (which it probably does), you must determine which port addresses are being used by other devices on your computer, then set the card to an unused port address. Table 3-2 shows port addresses typically used by various

Port Address	Device
1F0 - 1F8	AT hard disk (MFM type) controller and some floppy disk controllers
200 - 20F	Game adapter
230 - 23F	Bus mouse
278 - 27F	LPT2 (or LPT3, if used)
2E0 - 2EF	COM4
2F8 - 2FF	COM2
320 - 33F	XT (MFM type) and some SCSI hard disk controllers
340 - 35F	Some SCSI hard disk controllers
378 - 37F	LPT1 (or LPT2, if LPT3 used)
3B0 - 3BF	Monochrome or Hercules display adapters (or LPT1, if LPT3 used)
3C0 - 3CF	EGA and VGA display adapters
3D0 - 3DF	CGA and MCGA display adapters (or EGA/VGA in color video modes)
3E8 - 3EF	COM3
3F0 - 3F7	Floppy disk controller
3F8 - 3FF	COM1

Port Addresses and the Devices That Typically Use Them
Table 3-2.

devices. Do not set your network card to an address range that is partially or wholly used by another device on your system. Most computers have a parallel and a serial port, so it is usually safe to assume that addresses 378-37F (LPT1 parallel port) and 3F8-3FF (COM1 serial port) are in use. Use this table as a rough guide only; your system will not use all these devices or port addresses.

A port address range of 300-30F is often a good choice.

Base Memory Address

The *base memory address* setting, if your network card has it, determines the starting address in the computer's upper memory area that the

Selecting and Installing Network Hardware

network card will use. Not all network cards use a base memory address (Ethernet does not, unless you are using the card in a computer with no disk drives, and have installed a *remote boot PROM* that enables the computer to boot from the hard disk in another computer). If your card has this setting (ARCnet usually does), you must find an unused area in your computer's upper memory area, and set the switches to this address. If you have the Microsoft Diagnostics program available, look for upper memory areas marked as "available" (see "Determining Card Settings" for more information on this program).

Base memory addresses, like base I/O port addresses, are usually expressed in hexadecimal notation, and the card uses a range of addresses. Table 3-3 shows typical uses of the upper memory area, including areas that might be available.

Memory addresses D000-D07F or E000-E07F are good choices in many systems.

If you are using the EMM386 expanded memory manager to manage the upper memory area of your computer, the upper memory locations (if any) that your network card is using should be excluded from use by EMM386. This is accomplished by adding the X= switch, along with the memory addresses, to the DEVICE command that loads EMM386. This command line is located in your CONFIG.SYS file, and it can be

Memory Address	Typical Use
A000 - AFFF	EGA and VGA display (high resolution)
B000 - B7FF	MDA and Hercules display
B800 - BFFF	EGA and VGA (text/low resolution), Hercules, CGA
C000 - C7FF	VGA, EGA, 8514/A display, or disk controller ROM
C800 - CBFF	8514/A display
CC00 - DBFF	Free (unless used by expanded memory page frames)
DC00 - DFFF	Free (unless used by SCSI device)
E000 - EFFF	Free (except on PS/2 and some others)
F000 - FFFF	System ROM BIOS

Uses of the Upper Memory Area
Table 3-3.

modified using any unformatted (DOS or ASCII) text file editor like the DOS Editor or Notepad in Windows. For example, if your card uses the upper memory area E000-E07F, exclude this area by adding the following line to your CONFIG.SYS file:

```
DEVICE=C:\WINDOWS\EMM386.EXE X=E000-E07F
```

NOTE: If you have not yet upgraded to DOS 5, it is highly recommended that you do so before installing Windows for Workgroups. This version of DOS is designed to work with Windows for Workgroups, and it provides many memory-management tools essential for optimizing your computer's performance (see Chapter 4 for more information on optimizing your computer to run Windows for Workgroups).

Node Address

Each network interface card must have a unique *node address* to identify the source and destination of the packets sent out on the network cables. Some cards have this address permanently set (typically Ethernet), while others use switches that are accessible from the back of the computer with the card installed. The only requirement for this setting is that no two cards in your LAN share the same node address; the numbers that you choose are completely arbitrary. On cards with this setting, record the address chosen on a label and stick it on the card's mounting bracket so that it can be read from outside the computer.

Determining Card Settings

The cards you purchase for your LAN may not have all of the settings discussed in this section or may have additional settings (for example, there might be a jumper setting for the type of coax cable used). Be sure to record the settings for each network interface card in your LAN notebook.

To determine the settings that are right for each computer, consult the documentation for the network card used and the other cards installed in the computer. Also, watch the messages that appear on the screen

Selecting and Installing Network Hardware

when you boot the computer, and run a diagnostics program that reports system information such as IRQ numbers, I/O port addresses, and upper memory usage. If you have Windows 3.1 installed, run the Microsoft Diagnostics (MSD.EXE) program that is included with Windows and some other Microsoft products. You can also install Windows for Workgroups to get the MSD utility.

To run the Microsoft Diagnostics program, type **msd** from the DOS command line. From the main menu, choose the Memory, IRQ Status, LPT Ports, and COM Ports options (and browse the other options) to gain much valuable information about your system. Other software products that might give you the necessary system information include QuarterDeck's Manifest, The Norton Utilities, and PC Tools.

A Network Shopping List

For whichever protocol and topology you choose for your LAN, refer to the following shopping list as a general guide when purchasing your hardware. Obtain some knowledgeable advice about the specific network hardware and its requirements before you buy it—preferably from the dealer from whom you purchase it. If you later encounter problems with setting up your LAN, a knowledgeable dealer can be an invaluable source of advice. In general, to set up a small Windows for Workgroups LAN you will need the following:

✦ Network interface cards, one per computer. Choose the faster 16-bit cards if your budget allows it.

✦ Hubs (active or passive) if you are using star topology.

✦ Tee connectors if you are using coaxial bus topology.

✦ Terminators for the two ends of a bus and any unused connectors on a passive hub (active hubs usually do not need terminators). Some twisted-pair cards have an optional built-in terminator (ask the dealer about this if you are using twisted-pair).

✦ The correct number of cables of the *exact* type required for the topology chosen. Your LAN plan should enable you to purchase the correct lengths of cable. Particularly if you are buying ready-made cables in standard lengths, you might need some couplers (or barrel connectors) to join lengths of cable between nodes.

✦ Tools for cutting, stripping, and fastening cable connectors if you choose to make up your own network cabling (this is not recommended, since the chance of having at least one bad connection is high, and troubleshooting bad cables can more than offset the higher cost of purchasing ready-made cables). Additional tools to have on hand include screwdrivers, nut drivers, tweezers or hemostats for moving jumpers (if your fingers are less than nimble), a mirror and flashlight for inspecting obscure spots (like the back of a computer without moving it), pliers for tight BNC connectors, and possibly tools for routing cables through ceilings and walls and fastening them out of the way.

Installing Your Network Hardware

Once you've completed your LAN plan, you can begin purchasing and installing your network hardware. This involves the following steps:

1. Decide which protocol (usually Ethernet or ARCnet) and which topology (bus or star) you want to use for your LAN. Show the drawing of your office layout to the dealer from whom you are purchasing the network hardware. Make sure that the topology you choose is appropriate for the distances involved; don't use any cable runs that exceed the maximum distances listed in the card's documentation.

2. Run the cables to the computers in your LAN. If your workgroup is spread out in different rooms, running the cables might be a big job, so allow plenty of time to accomplish this task.

3. Configure the network interface card for each workgroup computer. Read the previous section, "Network Interface Cards," in this chapter, as well as the documentation for the network cards, and refer to the information you gathered about each workgroup computer and recorded in your LAN plan. The default settings that the network card came with might work on a computer with few devices. If your computer has only one parallel and one serial port and no special cards, you might try just plugging in the network card as is.

4. Install each card in its computer at a time when nobody will be working on the machine for some time (for example, in the evening, or on Saturday). Turn off the computer, but leave it

Selecting and Installing Network Hardware

plugged into the power outlet so that the computer case will be grounded (this is important to prevent static discharge damage to the electronics). Remove the screws and take off the computer's cover. Blow out excessive dust with an unheated blow dryer or a grounded vacuum cleaner, if necessary. Locate an appropriate slot (8-bit or 16-bit) on the system board, and remove the metal plate from the back of the case. Touch the metal case to discharge any static, then carefully insert the network card in the slot, making sure that it seats fully and that the notch in its rear bracket lines up with the screw hole in the rear of the case. Fasten the card's mounting bracket to the case and place the cover back on, but don't reinstall the screws until you have tested the computer.

5. Boot up the computer and run the diagnostic utility if one came with the card. Try running some applications, print something, use the mouse, and test the modem, if any. If you receive any error messages, extra beeps, or other strange behavior, refer to "Troubleshooting Your LAN" later in this chapter. Otherwise, replace the screws in the cover and move on to the next computer. Installing the cards can be spread out over any period of time, since the installed cards should not affect the functioning of the computers.

NOTE: Let the users know that you have installed the network cards so they will know who to come to if a problem occurs.

6. Connect the cables between the computers, adding terminators and hubs where necessary.
7. Install and configure the network operating system, Windows for Workgroups. This step is covered in the remaining chapters in this book.

Troubleshooting Your Network Hardware

Most problems with the network hardware are due to conflicts between the network card and other devices in the computer. These conflicts can usually be resolved by modifying the settings on the network card.

A basic principle of troubleshooting is to make only *one* change at a time. When you follow this principle, you always know exactly which change in a setting produced which effect on the system. Usually, you should undo your last change before making another. Another basic principle is to write down each change as you make it. This provides you with a written record of what you've tried—a troubleshooting audit trail.

✦ Run the diagnostics program (if any) that came with your network interface card.

✦ Look for conflicts between the network card's settings and other devices in the computer. Reread "Network Card Settings" earlier in this chapter. If you don't have Windows 3.1 on your computer, you might need to install Windows for Workgroups so that you can run the MSD program (see Chapter 4 for instructions on installing Windows for Workgroups).

✦ If you suspect that the network card is conflicting with another device but are unable to determine which one, try removing all nonessential cards but the network card, then add them back one at a time until the problem reappears.

✦ If the expanded memory manager EMM386.EXE is being used, verify that EMM386 is not attempting to use the upper memory locations (if any) that the network card is using. These memory areas can be excluded from use by EMM386 with the X= switch in your CONFIG.SYS file. See "Base Memory Address" earlier in this chapter for instructions on using this switch.

✦ Check for loose or missing jumpers on the network card. Activate each individual switch by moving it back and forth. Sometimes they end up somewhere between on and off, making a poor connection.

✦ If there are diagnostic lights on the back of your network card, observe them and refer to the documentation for instructions on their use.

✦ Make sure the network card is firmly seated in the system board slot, and that the mounting screw is in place. If the gold contacts on the edge of the card have been handled, clean them with a pencil eraser before inserting the card in the slot.

Selecting and Installing Network Hardware

◆ Inspect each cable connection to make sure that it is not loose. Verify that the proper terminators have been used wherever the topology requires them. If your card has more than one type of cable connector on the back of it, verify that you have configured the card to use the correct one.

◆ If you have an ohmmeter available, the individual cables can be tested for continuity. There should be very little resistance between the two center leads and between the two twist-lock connectors on coaxial cables. Twisted-pair wire can be similarly tested for continuity between corresponding contacts on the two ends. Terminators can also be tested for the correct resistance. Typically, ARCnet coaxial cable requires 93 ohm terminators, and Ethernet coaxial requires 50 ohm terminators. Twisted-pair typically requires 100 ohm resistance between pairs of terminator contacts. Consult your card's documentation for the resistance value and the contacts to check.

◆ After you are sure that the card's settings are correct, try swapping the network cards between the computer having a problem and one that is functioning correctly. If the problem moves to the other computer, you may have a bad card. You will have to adjust the settings on the two cards unless they are identically configured.

◆ Call the dealer who sold you the network hardware and ask for technical assistance. Have your LAN notebook in front of you. The list of the system's hardware and the network card settings used will be needed by the technician that you talk to.

◆ As a last resort, hire a network consultant to visit your site and help you.

CHAPTER

4

INSTALLING AND CONFIGURING WINDOWS FOR WORKGROUPS

Now that you have installed your networking hardware, you are ready to install (or set up) Windows for Workgroups itself. This is a quick and painless process, since the Setup program does most of the work for you.

This chapter covers the software and hardware requirements of Windows for Workgroups, running the Setup program, and some customizing and optimizing procedures that you can use to make Windows for Workgroups fit your needs. A troubleshooting section at the end of this chapter guides you through solving many of the problems that might arise during the installation process.

Requirements for Running Windows for Workgroups

Before starting installation, verify that each computer in your workgroup has the hardware and software necessary for supporting Windows for Workgroups. Included with your Windows for Workgroups package is a "Hardware Compatibility List," which lists the brands of hardware components that have been tested and approved for running Windows for Workgroups. If your hardware is listed, or is 100 percent compatible with hardware on the list, it is capable of running Windows for Workgroups. In some cases, the manufacturer of noncompatible hardware can provide you with software that enables you to use the device with Windows for Workgroups.

NOTE: In the following list of hardware and software required for running Windows for Workgroups, the minimum disk space requirements do not allow for a full installation including optional components, support for additional networks, and multiple printers.

Verify that each computer has the following:

♦ At least one floppy disk drive—high density is recommended. Be sure that the Windows for Workgroups disks you purchase are the correct type for your floppy drive.

♦ DOS version 3.3 or later. DOS 5 or later is highly recommended, because it provides the enhanced support for running Windows for Workgroups. If you don't know what version of DOS you have, type **ver** at the DOS command line.

♦ A computer with an 80386 or later processor to run in 386 enhanced mode, or an 80286 or later processor to run in standard mode. In order to share its resources (for example, a printer or a

Installing and Configuring Windows for Workgroups

hard disk directory), a computer must run in 386 enhanced mode. Standard mode only allows a computer to use the resources of others. Windows for Workgroups cannot run on earlier computers which use 8086 and 8088 processors.

◆ At least 3.6MB of memory for running in 386 enhanced mode (4MB or more is recommended) and 1MB or more of memory for standard mode (2MB or more is recommended). These figures include 640K of conventional memory and assume that all memory above 1MB is extended (not expanded) memory. *Expanded memory* located on a special memory-expansion board can be used, but it is in addition to the above figures. (See Figure 3-1 in Chapter 3 for a diagram of the various types of computer memory.)

◆ At least 9.5MB of space available on your hard disk (14.5MB is recommended) for running Windows in either 386 enhanced mode or standard mode. If you are upgrading a 386 computer from Windows 3.1 to Windows for Workgroups, you can get by with 3.5MB of free disk space, but at least 8.5MB is recommended.

◆ A supported display adapter. Check the "Hardware Compatibility List" for this. A VGA display is recommended for this colorful graphical environment.

◆ A network interface card for each computer in your workgroup, plus the appropriate cables and other network hardware required by the particular network protocol and topology that you choose. (See Chapter 3 for details.)

◆ A printer listed on the "Hardware Compatibility List," or the use of a shared printer.

◆ A mouse listed on the "Hardware Compatibility List." (A mouse is not absolutely required for running Windows for Workgroups, but is highly recommended.)

◆ A Hayes, MultiTech, or Trail Blazer modem (or a modem compatible with one of these) if you plan to use Terminal, the Windows for Workgroups communications application.

◆ A sound card if you plan to take advantage of the sound features in Windows for Workgroups.

Running Windows for Workgroups Setup

Now that you have verified that you have the minimum requirements for running Windows for Workgroups, take some time to familiarize yourself with the Setup program before you proceed with installation. It will help you install Windows for Workgroups to better fit your needs.

Tasks Performed by Setup

The Setup program performs many tasks for you. You might not be aware of many of these changes, depending on the options you choose in the Setup program. When you run Setup, it performs the following functions:

✦ Analyzes your system to learn what hardware you have, including your network card and its settings.

✦ Copies the appropriate files from the Windows for Workgroups disks to your hard disk, while expanding them from their compressed form.

✦ Modifies the Windows configuration files (SYSTEM.INI and WIN.INI) to fit your particular system.

✦ Searches for Windows applications on your hard disk, and creates *program-item icons* (small graphical symbols that represent an application that can be run or a document that can be edited) for the ones it finds. After Setup is completed, you will be able to run these applications by double-clicking on their icons.

✦ Sets up each existing non-Windows application (not written specifically to run in Windows) that it recognizes on your hard disk, making a Program Information File (PIF) and a program-item icon for each.

The PIF enables Windows to run the application efficiently, even though the application was not designed to run under Windows. (If you have created PIFs for a previous version of Windows, Setup will ask you if you want to use them or create new ones.) You can start non-Windows applications running the same way you start Windows applications, once they have a PIF and icon.

Installing and Configuring Windows for Workgroups

✦ Modifies your CONFIG.SYS and AUTOEXEC.BAT files when you use Express Setup or when you use Custom Setup and allow these modifications to be made.

✦ Restarts your system, if you choose to let it do so. (In order to make any changes in your AUTOEXEC.BAT and CONFIG.SYS files take effect and to connect to others on your Windows for Workgroups LAN, your machine should be restarted after running Setup.)

Upgrading from Windows 3.0 or 3.1

If you already have Windows 3.0 or 3.1 on your hard disk, Setup gives you the option of upgrading the existing Windows software to Windows for Workgroups. Unless you have a specific need to maintain the older version of Windows, you should choose to upgrade it. When you choose to upgrade, Setup preserves your existing Windows settings, program groups, and program items while adding the networking abilities and enhancements of Windows for Workgroups. When you choose not to upgrade, you lose all the customization that you have done to Windows, as well as invite potential problems such as missing device drivers.

CAUTION: If you already have Windows on your system, you should back up all data files and programs that you have added to your Windows directories before running Setup.

When you choose to upgrade your existing Windows software, Setup does the following:

✦ Preserves existing Windows settings for your computer, monitor, mouse, keyboard, language, and the associated device drivers. (A *device driver* is a piece of software that allows a particular hardware device, like a printer, to work with your computer and Windows.)

✦ Preserves existing Program Manager groups, including any new groups that you have created, and any program items that you have added to Program Manager groups.

✦ Preserves any LOADHIGH commands in your AUTOEXEC.BAT file, and DEVICEHIGH commands in your CONFIG.SYS file, keeping them in their original order in the file. (LOADHIGH and DEVICEHIGH are DOS commands for starting memory-resident programs in the upper memory area.)

✦ Updates any existing Windows device drivers to the new version if one is available.

✦ Preserves installed device drivers that were not originally supplied with Windows. (There might be an upgraded version of the device driver supplied with Windows for Workgroups. Choose the README program item in the Program Manager's Main group after Windows for Workgroups is up and running, for more information.)

How Setup Modifies Your System Files

When you run Setup, several changes are made to your CONFIG.SYS and AUTOEXEC.BAT files (unless you choose not to have these changes made when running Custom Setup).

Changes to AUTOEXEC.BAT   Setup makes the following changes to your AUTOEXEC.BAT file:

✦ The name of the directory in which the Windows for Workgroups files is located is added to your PATH command. This directory name is typically WINDOWS (unless you chose a different name during Setup).

✦ The SMARTDRV.EXE command is added (if you have at least 2MB of extended memory). This command starts the Windows disk-caching program which uses extended memory to temporarily store information on its way to or from your hard disk. SMARTDRV makes Windows for Workgroups run much faster and is highly recommended.

✦ The commands necessary for connecting your computer to the Windows for Workgroups LAN are added. Normally this is just C:\WINDOWS\NET START if C:\WINDOWS is your Windows directory.

✦ The TEMP *environment variable* is assigned to the TEMP directory (which is created if necessary), unless this variable has already been

Installing and Configuring Windows for Workgroups

assigned. (Many applications use the directory represented by the variable name TEMP, for storing files that are deleted when the application no longer needs them.)

Changes to CONFIG.SYS   Setup makes the following changes to your CONFIG.SYS file:

◆ A line is added to force SMARTDRIVE to use double-buffering, if your hard disk controller requires it. This line has the form:

```
DEVICE=C:\WINDOWS\SMARTDRV.EXE /DOUBLE_BUFFER
```

◆ A line is added that loads the extended memory manager, HIMEM.SYS (unless this has already been done). This line has the form:

```
DEVICE=C:\WINDOWS\HIMEM.SYS
```

◆ The RAMDRIVE.SYS and EMM386.EXE commands (if they exist) are updated to use the versions supplied with Windows for Workgroups.

◆ Lines for the network interface card device driver and the network protocol are added.

◆ The line that loads a Microsoft or other mouse device driver is updated.

◆ Lines for any incompatible device drivers are deleted.

◆ If you have an EGA display or a Mouse Systems mouse, the device driver line is updated or added.

◆ If you have a 386MAX command line, it is modified by adding an appropriate parameter.

Choosing Your Setup Method

There are two kinds of Setup: Express Setup and Custom Setup. When you run Setup, you are asked to choose the method that you want to use for installing Windows for Workgroups. The following discussions are intended to help you decide which method is most appropriate for you.

Express Setup

Because Express Setup is the easiest to use and does most of the work for you, it is recommended for most users. Express Setup automatically identifies your hardware and software, then updates files and configures Windows for optimum performance. Express Setup also sets up most or all of your existing applications so that they can be run from Windows. (Later, from Windows, you can add any applications that were not set up or delete any that you do not want set up.) If you don't have enough hard disk space for a complete setup, Express Setup will search for other local drives on which to install itself. It also gives you the option of doing a partial setup, which leaves out some optional Windows components (such as screen savers). If you have a previous version of Windows on your computer, Express Setup sets up your currently installed printer automatically.

You need to know the following about your system when you use Express Setup:

✦ The name that you want to give your computer. This name is used to identify your computer to others on your Windows for Workgroups LAN, and can be up to 15 characters long.

✦ The name of your workgroup, which is the set of computers with which your computer will be associated. This name should be different from your computer name, and can be up to 15 characters long.

✦ The type of printer you will be using—either one directly connected to your computer or one shared by another computer on the LAN (choose None if no printer will be used).

✦ The port that your printer is connected to. Usually this is a parallel printer port such as LPT1 or LPT2, a serial port such as COM1 or COM2, or a port on another computer on the LAN.

✦ The type of network interface card installed in your computer. (If you need to use more than one card, use Custom Setup or add the second one later, using the Network option in the Control Panel.)

✦ The settings that you chose for your network interface card, including the IRQ number, the base I/O port, and the base memory

Installing and Configuring Windows for Workgroups

address in upper memory. (See Chapter 3 and your LAN notebook for details.)

✦ The type of any other network that your computer will be running along with Windows for Workgroups. Other networks supported include Novell NetWare and Microsoft LAN Manager.

Custom Setup

Custom Setup gives you more control over the way Windows for Workgroups is set up, but it requires you to know much more about your hardware and software. Use this method only if you have special needs. Typical reasons for using Custom Setup are to modify proposed changes to your AUTOEXEC.BAT and CONFIG.SYS files (or to prevent any changes), and to choose which optional Windows for Workgroups files are left off your hard disk to conserve disk space. Custom Setup also lists the hardware and software that it detects on your system and allows you to modify the list. In addition, you are given more control over which of your existing applications are set up, and how your printer is set up.

When you use Custom Setup, you are asked to provide information about the following:

✦ The directory in which to store the Windows for Workgroups files (C:\WINDOWS is recommended).

✦ The type of computer on which you are setting up Windows for Workgroups.

✦ The type of display adapter and monitor you have (for example, VGA or Super VGA).

✦ The type of mouse you have. You don't absolutely have to have a mouse, but you should have one to take full advantage of the Windows graphical user interface.

✦ The keyboard and layout you are using.

✦ The language you are using.

✦ The type of network interface card installed in your computer.

✦ The settings that you chose for your network interface card, including the IRQ number, the base I/O port, and the base memory address in upper memory (refer to the settings that you recorded in your LAN notebook).

If you need to connect your computer to more than one type of network protocol or topology, you can install up to four network interface cards in your computer (see Chapter 3 for more information on the various network protocols and topologies).

◆ The type of network that your computer will be running in addition to Windows for Workgroups, if any. Other networks supported include Novell NetWare and Microsoft LAN Manager.

◆ The type of printer you will be using—either directly connected to your computer or shared with other computers on the LAN (choose None if no printer will be used).

◆ The port that your printer is connected to. Usually this is a parallel printer port such as LPT1 or LPT2, a serial port such as COM1 or COM2, or a port on another computer on the LAN.

◆ The applications on your hard disk that you want to run under Windows for Workgroups. You can run most of your existing applications even if they were not specifically designed for the Windows environment.

◆ Any changes that you want to make to your AUTOEXEC.BAT and CONFIG.SYS files. For example, you might want to remove a memory-resident program that you won't use with Windows for Workgroups, or add a command that will start Windows for Workgroups running when you turn on your computer.

◆ Any optional Windows components and accessories that you want Setup to install. You might want to omit some of these to conserve disk space.

◆ Virtual memory settings, if you are going to run Windows for Workgroups in 386 enhanced mode (which is necessary for sharing your computer's resources).

◆ The name that you want to give your computer. This name is used to identify your computer to others on your Windows for Workgroups LAN, and can be up to 15 characters long.

◆ The name of your workgroup, which is the set of computers with which your computer will be associated. This name should be

Installing and Configuring Windows for Workgroups

different from your computer name, and can be up to 15 characters long.

Installing Windows for Workgroups with Setup

Now that you have decided whether you will use Express Setup or Custom Setup, you are almost ready to install Windows for Workgroups. But first, take the time to disable any DOS screen saver that you use, since these can cause problems when running Setup. Also, pop-up message programs, like those used to notify you about your print jobs, can cause Setup to fail, and should be turned off. An easy way to disable a memory-resident program is to insert a REM command at the beginning of the line in your AUTOEXEC.BAT or CONFIG.SYS file that starts the program. Use any unformatted text editor (like the DOS Editor in DOS 5) for this task. Then reboot your computer and you are ready to run Setup.

To install Windows for Workgroups with the Setup program:

1. Insert Disk 1 from your Windows for Workgroups package into a floppy drive.
2. Make that drive the current one by typing its letter followed by a colon (for example **a:**), then press (Enter).
3. Type **setup** and press (Enter).
4. Follow the instructions on the screen.

When you see the screen shown in Figure 4-1, press (Enter) to use Express Setup, or **c** to use Custom Setup.

You can press (F3) to quit Setup at any point during the process, or get online help by pressing (F1). If you have a previous version of Windows on your system, Setup asks you to specify whether you want to upgrade it to Windows for Workgroups or to install the new software in a separate directory, as shown in Figure 4-2.

Setup prompts you when it's time to insert the next disk in the floppy drive and then requests that you type the user, computer, and workgroup names. Next, it prompts you for printer information. (If you are using Express Setup to upgrade a previous Windows installation, your existing printer is automatically set up.) If you are using Custom

```
Windows for Workgroups Setup
────────────────────────────────────────

    Windows for Workgroups provides two Setup methods:

    Express Setup (Recommended)
    Express Setup relies on Setup to make decisions,
    so setting up Windows is quick and easy.

        To use Express Setup, press ENTER.


    Custom Setup
    Custom Setup is for experienced computer users who
    want to control how Windows is set up. To use this Setup method,
    you should know how to use a mouse with Windows.

        To use Custom Setup, press C.

    For details about both Setup methods, press F1.


  ENTER=Express Setup   C=Custom Setup   F1=Help   F3=Exit
```

Setup requires you to choose the Express or Custom method
Figure 4-1.

Setup, you are given a chance to view and modify several other configuration items.

Once the Windows for Workgroups software is completely installed on your hard disk, you are given the opportunity to run a tutorial that gives you practice in using the mouse and some basic Windows

```
Windows for Workgroups Setup
────────────────────────────────────────

    Setup has found a previous version of Microsoft Windows on your hard
    disk in the path shown below. It is recommended that you upgrade this
    previous version to Windows for Workgroups version 3.1.

        • To upgrade, press ENTER.

    If necessary, you can keep your older version of Windows and add
    this new version to your system. Press the BACKSPACE key to erase
    the path shown, and then type a new path for version 3.1.

        • When the correct path is shown below, press ENTER.

    C:\WINDOWS

    Note: if you set up this version in a new directory instead of
    upgrading, you will not maintain any of your desktop settings or any
    Program Manager groups and icons you set up. Also, you must make sure
    that only the correct path is listed in PATH in your AUTOEXEC.BAT file


  ENTER=Continue   F1=Help   F3=Exit
```

Setup has found a previous version of Windows
Figure 4-2.

techniques. (You can run this tutorial later by choosing it from the Program Manager's Help menu.)

After Windows is up and running, you might want to choose (double-click on) the README icon for the most current information on Windows for Workgroups, including software and hardware compatibility issues, and the names of other information files available for viewing or printing.

Starting Windows for Workgroups

To start Windows for Workgroups, type **win** and press Enter from the DOS command line. You can have Windows for Workgroups start automatically each time you boot your computer by placing this WIN command on a new line at the end of your AUTOEXEC.BAT file.

Standard or 386 Enhanced Mode

Windows for Workgroups starts running in the mode (standard or 386 enhanced) that it determines is most efficient for your computer. (To find out which mode Windows for Workgroups is running in, choose About from the Program Manager's Help menu.)

Standard mode is the lower operational level of Windows for Workgroups. When running in standard mode, extended memory is available and you can switch among several Windows applications running simultaneously. Standard mode allows you to use the resources of other computers on the LAN, but you cannot share your computer's resources with others. If your computer has an 80286 processor, Windows for Workgroups can only run in standard mode.

The higher level *386 enhanced mode* uses your hard disk to provide additional memory to applications; this is called *virtual* memory. It also provides greater flexibility in the way non-Windows applications can be run, and allows you to share your computer's resources with others on the LAN (as well as use the resources of others).

If your computer has an 80386 or later processor with enough memory available, you can run Windows for Workgroups in either mode by adding the /3 or /s switch to the WIN command. The next section discusses conditions under which you might want to specify the mode in which Windows for Workgroups runs, rather than letting that choice be made for you.

Specifying a Windows for Workgroups Mode

When you start Windows for Workgroups on a 386 (or later) computer with less than 4MB of memory, it starts in standard mode unless you specify otherwise. If your 386 has at least 3.6MB of memory, you can make Windows for Workgroups run in 386 enhanced mode to increase the number of applications that you can run simultaneously. The trade-off for the increased flexibility of running in 386 enhanced mode in this case is slower performance, because you have less than the normal amount of memory required for this mode.

To force Windows for Workgroups to start in 386 enhanced mode, add the /3 switch when you start it, as follows:

win/3

You might want to force Windows for Workgroups to run in standard mode if you are experiencing hardware compatibility problems when running in 386 enhanced mode. This can allow you to work in Windows for Workgroups while you troubleshoot the problem, but you won't be able to share your computer's resources.

To force Windows for Workgroups to start in standard mode, add the /s switch when you start it, as follows:

win/s

Starting an Application Automatically

If you always start a particular application after starting Windows for Workgroups, you can have it start automatically each time Windows for Workgroups starts. There are two ways to do this:

✦ Add the application's program item to the Program Manager's Startup group (drag the program's icon to the Startup group window or icon).

Installing and Configuring Windows for Workgroups

◆ Add the application's program filename (including the path, if needed) after the command used to start Windows for Workgroups (after the /s or /3 switch, if either is used). For example, to start the Notepad application at the same time as Windows for Workgroups, you could type:

win notepad.exe

If your application allows you to include the name of a document to open when it is started, you can add this to the command. For example, to open AUTOEXEC.BAT when Notepad is started, you could type:

win notepad.exe c:\autoexec.bat

If a document is associated with an application, you can just add the document name, leaving off the application name. When an *association* exists between an application and the documents created by it, the application is automatically started when one of the documents (with a particular filename extension) is chosen. Associations can be created with the Associate option in File Manager's File menu.

To see a complete list of the switches that can be included with the WIN command, type **win/?** at the DOS prompt. Some switches are used for troubleshooting and are covered in the troubleshooting section later in this chapter.

Logging on to Windows for Workgroups

Each time you start Windows for Workgroups, you are prompted to log on (unless you chose not to log on the first time you started Windows for Workgroups after running Setup). *Logging on* consists of typing your logon name and password in the Windows for Workgroups logon dialog box, shown here:

Your logon name (which is not necessarily the same as the computer name) can be any name that you choose to identify yourself with, such as your first name, initials, or a nickname. Your password, which is never shown as you type it (asterisks appear in place of the typed characters), can be any combination of 14 or fewer characters (numbers and upper- and lowercase letters). Until you type the correct password, you are prevented from using the resources that others in your workgroup are sharing. Choose a password that you can easily remember, but if security is important, change it regularly and don't use your name or initials as a password.

More than one person can log on to the same computer (but only one at a time); each must use a different logon name and password. The first time a user logs on to the LAN on a particular computer, a *password list* file is created under the logon name. This file stores the logon password as well as any passwords required for access to shared resources on the LAN. It is "locked" when the user logs off so that others do not have access to the passwords. Since access to the resources on your Windows for Workgroups LAN can be controlled by passwords, each person using a particular computer might have access to a different set of LAN resources.

NOTE: Windows for Workgroups security features are not as hard to defeat as those of the larger client-server LANs, so it might not be prudent to store very sensitive documents in shared directories on a Windows for Workgroups LAN.

See Chapter 5 for more information on sharing resources and Chapter 6 for information on connecting to and using the resources of others.

Installing and Configuring Windows for Workgroups

Customizing Network Settings

The Network option in the Control Panel (located in the Program Manager's Main group) enables you to customize your Windows for Workgroups connections in various ways. The following sections briefly discuss these options. You can also view the online help for the Network option by choosing the Help button available in dialog boxes.

Click on the Network icon in the Control Panel to get the Network Settings dialog box shown in Figure 4-3.

In the Network Settings dialog box you can change your computer name, create a new workgroup or change the workgroup your computer belongs to, change the comment that appears after your computer name, disable all sharing on your computer, and adjust the percentage of your processor's time that is devoted to sharing your resources.

Changing Your Computer Name

In the Computer Name text box, type the new name assigned to your computer. This name must uniquely identify your computer (no other

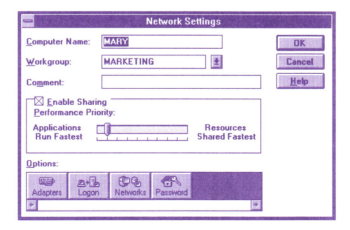

Network Settings dialog box
Figure 4-3.

computer or workgroup can have it). It can be up to 15 characters long. You can use letters, numbers, and the following characters:

! # $ % & ( ) - . @ ^ _ ' ~

Changing Your Workgroup

To create a new workgroup name for your computer to belong to, type the name in the Workgroup text box. The name can have up to 15 characters, using the same set of characters as for your computer name.

To change to a different workgroup, open the drop-down list by choosing the down arrow to the right of the Workgroup text box, and choose a workgroup name from the list.

Adding a Comment

You can create a comment that describes your computer, if you want to. This comment appears next to your computer name in the dialog boxes used to connect to other computers in the workgroup. This description can be up to 48 characters long.

Enabling and Disabling Sharing

If you want to disable all sharing from your computer, clear the Enable Sharing check box by clicking on it. Click on it again to enable sharing. When this option is disabled, the Performance Priority option is also disabled.

Adjusting Performance Priority

The Performance Priority option adjusts the relative speed at which your applications run versus the speed at which others are able to use your computer's resources. When you drag the pointer toward the left your applications run faster, but people using your computer's resources will notice a decrease in performance. When you drag the pointer toward the right your applications run more slowly, but performance is increased for others using your resources. If your computer is primarily used to share resources, move the pointer closer to Resources Shared Fastest.

Changing Logon Settings

Choose the Logon button at the bottom of the Network Settings dialog box to get the Logon Settings dialog box shown here:

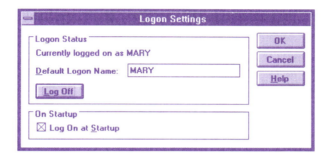

If you are currently logged on, you can choose the Log Off button to log off the network. You are warned that logging off breaks any shared connections that exist. If you are not currently logged on, the logon dialog box appears. Type your logon name and password in the appropriate boxes and choose OK.

You can also change the default logon name that appears in the logon dialog box by typing the name in the Default Logon Name text box in the Logon Settings dialog box.

To specify whether or not users should be prompted to log on when starting Windows for Workgroups, check or clear the Log On at Startup check box.

Additional Options

Additional options exist for specifying your network interface adapter settings (see "Your Network Hardware Does Not Work" in the troubleshooting section for instructions on using this feature). You can also specify networks other than Windows for Workgroups that your computer is using. Other networks supported include Novell NetWare and Microsoft LAN Manager.

Troubleshooting Windows for Workgroups

This section covers problems that you might encounter while running Setup or when first starting Windows for Workgroups after completing Setup. If you do have problems with Windows for Workgroups, look in the following sections for a description of the problem that you are having. If you don't find a description of your problem, or if the suggested solutions don't solve your problem, look at the troubleshooting document discussed next and check the end of this section for additional resources.

Read SETUP.TXT

The file named SETUP.TXT contains information about problems that specific hardware and software might cause while running the Setup program, or when running Windows for Workgroups after it is set up. For instance, if you have a memory-resident program running when you start the Setup program, you might receive a message on your screen regarding potential problems. SETUP.TXT lists specific hardware and software that might cause problems and provides instructions on resolving the problems. If you encounter problems setting up Windows for Workgroups, read SETUP.TXT before running Setup again.

SETUP.TXT is located on Disk 1 of your Windows for Workgroups software or in your Windows directory if you completed Setup. If you completed Setup, and Windows for Workgroups runs, you can view this file using Notepad.

The Notepad application is an unformatted text editor located in the Program Manager's Accessories group. To start Notepad, double-click on its icon. To open the SETUP.TXT file, choose Open from Notepad's File menu, then type the filename in the File Name text box or choose the file from the list below the text box. Click on the OK button and maximize the window for easiest viewing.

If you cannot use Windows for Workgroups, you can view the SETUP.TXT file using any text editor (for example, the DOS Editor), or use the TYPE and MORE commands from the DOS command line, as follows:

1. Insert Disk 1 into your floppy disk drive (A is assumed; substitute your drive's actual letter), and type

Installing and Configuring Windows for Workgroups

type a:\setup.txt | more

2. Press any key to display one screenful of text at a time.
3. When you are ready, press Ctrl-C to cancel the file viewing and return to the DOS prompt.

Your Network Hardware Does Not Work

If you have a problem getting Windows for Workgroups up and running, there is a good chance that it is due to an improperly configured (or defective) network interface card, or a bad cable. Some signs of network hardware failure are

◆ You receive a message on your screen about a problem.

◆ Your system freezes up when starting or running Windows for Workgroups.

◆ You are unable to connect with other computers in your workgroup.

If you think that your network hardware has a problem, or are unable to find your problem described elsewhere, review "Troubleshooting Your Network Hardware" and "Network Card Settings" in Chapter 3 and try the following suggestions:

Check Cables and Terminators   Check every cable and terminator connection for tightness.

Check Seating of Network Interface Card   Verify that your network interface card is seated properly in its slot (with the screw in place on the rear bracket). Make sure that you have not inserted a 16-bit card in an 8-bit slot. (See Chapter 3 for an illustration of the two types of slots.)

Gather Documentation   Dig up all the documentation that you can find for your system and the devices installed on it. In particular, the documentation for your network card, mouse, I/O card, hard and floppy disk controller(s), internal modem card, video adapter card, and any other add-on cards would be helpful.

Observe Lights   If your card has lights (LEDs) on the back, observe them while you run the Setup program, and refer to the card's documentation for instructions on interpreting the lights.

Observe Screen Messages   Observe the messages that appear on your screen as you boot your computer (use the `Pause` key or `Ctrl`-`S` to control the scrolling). Watch for messages containing the word "Error," and if you see one, note the message just before it. If the commands in your AUTOEXEC.BAT file are not appearing on your screen, place a REM before the ECHO OFF command.

Disable "Remote Boot PROM"   Make sure that any "remote boot PROM" settings on your network interface card are disabled, unless your computer is set up as a *diskless workstation* that boots from another computer's hard disk.

Add an Exclude Statement in Your CONFIG.SYS   If your network card uses an address in upper memory (the base memory address), make sure that an "exclude" statement has been added to the line in CONFIG.SYS that loads EMM386 (if you use this memory manager). See "Base Memory Address" in Chapter 3 for instructions on adding this statement.

Select Connector   If your network card has more than one connector on the rear bracket, verify that you set the jumper that selects the one you're using.

Run Diagnostics   If a diagnostics program came with your network interface card, run the program and refer to the card's documentation. Then run the Microsoft Diagnostics (MSD) program (if Windows for Workgroups or Windows 3.1 is installed on your hard disk) for information about your system.

To run MSD, type **msd** at the DOS command line (don't run MSD from Windows). From MSD's main menu, choose the Memory, Mouse, IRQ Status, LPT Ports, and COM Ports options for information about upper memory area use, the hardware interrupts being used, and the port addresses in use. In addition, choose Memory Block Display from the Utilities menu for more detail on memory usage, and choose Print Report from the File menu if you want a hard copy of all your system information. As mentioned in Chapter 3, other possible sources for this

Installing and Configuring Windows for Workgroups

system information include QuarterDeck's Manifest, The Norton Utilities, and PC Tools.

Verify Network Adapter Driver   Verify that the network adapter driver is correct for your network adapter board. During installation, Setup attempts to determine the type of adapter board you are using and selects the driver accordingly. This selection process is less than perfect and may need correction. To do this, use the following steps:

1. Double-click on the Control Panel icon in the Program Manager's Main group.
2. Double-click on the Network icon.
3. Click on the Adapters button in the Network Settings dialog box.
4. Click on the Add button in the Network Adapters dialog box.
5. Scroll the list of network adapters until you see your card or one that is 100 percent compatible with your card. When you find your card, double-click on it. If you can't find your card, some good ones to try are:

    ✦ If you are using an 8-bit Ethernet card, try the NE1000 Compatible driver.

    ✦ If you are using a 16-bit Ethernet card, try the NE2000 Compatible driver.

    ✦ If you are using an ARCnet card, try either the ARCnet Compatible or SMC ARCNETPC drivers.

    If a software driver came on a disk with your board, select Unlisted or Updated Network Adapter from the list and then follow the instructions to insert the disk and install the correct driver.

6. When you have installed the new driver, click on OK or Close until you are back to the Control Panel window where you double-click on the Control menu box to close that window.

Change Conflicting Settings   Change any settings on your network interface card that might be conflicting with other devices in your system. Refer to the information gained from MSD or another diagnostic program, and from the documentation for your system's installed devices, to determine whether conflicts exist.

REMINDER: When troubleshooting, make only one change at a time and write down the changes as you make them. If the change doesn't help, undo it before making another.

If your network interface card uses software to configure it rather than jumpers and switches, run the configuration program that came with the card. (If you have an Intel EtherExpress 16 network card, simply follow the instructions described in the next paragraphs to reconfigure the card—Windows for Workgroups will automatically configure this card.)

Make Changes in Windows for Workgroups If you change any of your network interface card settings after Windows for Workgroups is set up, you must let Windows for Workgroups know of the change. To do so, follow these steps:

1. Double-click on the Control Panel icon in the Program Manager's Main group.
2. Double-click on the Network icon.
3. Click on the Adapters button in the Network Settings dialog box.
4. Click on the Setup button in the Adapter Settings dialog box.
5. Change the settings for your card in its dialog box. Your card might have additional settings in an "Advanced" dialog box. Choose the Help button for help with the card settings.
6. When you have made the changes you want to make, click on OK or Close until you are back to the Control Panel window, and double-click on its Control menu box to close that window.

Your Computer Locks Up in the First Part of Setup

One of the first things Setup does is identify your hardware. If Setup does not accomplish this task correctly, it might lock up (stop running)

Installing and Configuring Windows for Workgroups

during the first part of Setup. If this happens, restart Setup by typing

setup/i

This causes Setup to skip the hardware detection step and run Custom Setup. You can then choose the descriptions that match your hardware from the System Information screen.

Setup Stops After Completing the First Part

During the first part of the installation process Setup is running under DOS. When the progress bar reaches 100 percent, Setup starts running Windows for Workgroups. If Setup stops at the point of switching from DOS to Windows, one of the following might be the cause:

◆ Setup has incorrectly identified your hardware or software. Try restarting Setup and choosing Custom Setup. Check the descriptions in the System Information screen and correct any items that don't match your hardware or software.

◆ An incompatible memory-resident program is running at the same time as Setup. Look at SETUP.TXT (see the previous section, "Read SETUP.TXT") for information on specific memory-resident programs. Use the MEM/C command to see a list of the memory-resident programs running in your computer's memory. Memory-resident programs are usually loaded by a line in either your CONFIG.SYS or AUTOEXEC.BAT file, and can be temporarily disabled by inserting the REM command at the beginning of the line. Reboot after making changes to either of these two startup files.

◆ An application might be attempting to directly display a message on your screen. If you have a program that notifies you when your printing job is finished, for example, or if you are on a network with a message system, this might be your problem. You might need to log off your network while running Setup, or quit the conflicting application before running Setup again.

◆ You might be running a version of DOS prior to version 3.3 (version 5.0 is recommended). Type **ver** at the DOS command line to check your version of DOS.

Setup Keeps Asking for the Same Floppy Disk

If Setup keeps prompting you to insert a particular disk after you have already done so, one of the following might be the cause:

✦ A disk-caching program (for example, SMARTDRV) is running and reading files into memory. Locate and disable the command that starts the disk-caching program in your AUTOEXEC.BAT or CONFIG.SYS file, then reboot your computer (open the floppy drive door first) and restart Setup.

✦ Your computer might not be communicating properly with your floppy disk drive. Try adding the DRIVPARM command to your CONFIG.SYS file to solve this problem. The DRIVPARM command takes the following form,

drivparm=/d:x /f:y

where x = 0 or 1 (drive A: or B:), and y = 0 (360K drive), 1 (1.2MB drive), 2 (720K drive), or 7 (1.44MB drive). (For additional drive types, refer to the DRIVPARM command in your DOS manual.) Reboot after adding this line, and restart Setup.

A Hardware Device Doesn't Work

Setup automatically installs device drivers for hardware that it recognizes. If your device does not work in Windows for Workgroups, you might need to obtain an updated device driver for your hardware. Try the following sources:

✦ The dealer from whom you purchased your hardware device.

✦ The hardware manufacturer.

✦ The Microsoft Windows Driver Library (WDL), which is available via modem on CompuServe, GEnie, ON-Line, user-group bulletin-board services (BBSs) that are part of the APCUG network, and Microsoft's electronic downloading service at 206-936-6735. If you don't have a modem, you can call Microsoft Customer Support Services at 1-800-426-9400 to request drivers on disk.

Setup Warns You About a Memory-Resident Program

If you receive a message about a memory-resident program that is running during Setup, you should read SETUP.TXT, and possibly disable the memory-resident program. (See "Read SETUP.TXT," earlier in this chapter).

Windows Won't Start After Setup Finishes

If Setup appears to have successfully completed setting up Windows for Workgroups, but you are unable to get it running, look for the following causes:

✦ The wrong hardware settings were used for setting up your computer. If you used Express Setup, your hardware was not correctly identified by Setup. If you used Custom Setup, you specified your hardware incorrectly. To correct this problem, start Setup from your Windows directory and make the appropriate corrections to the hardware list.

✦ Your computer might be running a memory-resident program that is incompatible with Windows for Workgroups. (See the earlier discussion about incompatible memory-resident programs in "Setup Stops After Completing the First Part.")

✦ Your hardware settings are still incorrect. Run Setup again, using your Windows for Workgroups disks. This time, insert Disk 1 into your floppy drive and start Setup by typing

   setup /i

   This runs Custom Setup, skipping the hardware detection step, allowing you to specify your hardware in the "Hardware Configuration List."

✦ Try starting Windows for Workgroups by typing **win/b**. This switch causes Windows for Workgroups to create a file named BOOTLOG.TXT in which system startup messages are recorded as Windows for Workgroups attempts to start. Look at this file to discover where the startup process stopped. (View this unformatted text file the same way that you view SETUP.TXT, using a text editor or the TYPE and MORE commands.)

◆ Try starting Windows for Workgroups in standard mode and then in 386 enhanced mode. Start Windows for Workgroups in standard mode by typing

win /s

If Windows for Workgroups starts in standard mode, try starting it in 386 enhanced mode by typing

win /3

If you are unable to start Windows for Workgroups in 386 enhanced mode (assuming that your computer has the minimum requirements for running in this mode), see the next section.

You Can Run in Standard but Not 386 Enhanced Mode

If your 386 or newer computer won't start in 386 enhanced mode, try the following:

◆ Verify that there is at least 300K of free conventional memory and 3072K of free extended memory before starting Windows for Workgroups. Type **mem/c | more** to get this information, or run the MSD program. In addition, you need at least 2MB of space available on your hard disk.

◆ Try forcing Windows for Workgroups to start in 386 enhanced mode by typing

win /3

◆ Prevent Windows for Workgroups from searching the upper memory area for available memory space by typing

win /d:x

Installing and Configuring Windows for Workgroups

If Windows for Workgroups now starts in 386 enhanced mode, add the EMMExclude command to your SYSTEM.INI file. Use any text editor, such as the DOS Editor or Notepad, and add the following line under the [386Enh] section heading:

EMMExclude=A000-FFFF

✦ Give your hard disk, rather than Windows for Workgroups, control over hard disk interrupts by starting Windows for Workgroups with the following command:

win /d:v

If Windows for Workgroups now starts in 386 enhanced mode, add the VirtualHDirq=false command to your SYSTEM.INI file. Use a text editor as described before, but instead of the EMMExclude line, type

VirtualHDirq=false

Problems with Network Features

If you are able to run Windows for Workgroups, but have trouble with one of the networking features, look in the following sections for help.

None of the Network Features Is Available

If Windows for Workgroups is unable to start the networking part of the Windows for Workgroups operating system, you will see a message stating that you will not be able to use the network features. If you see this message when you start Windows for Workgroups, try the following:

✦ Verify that your computer has the minimum requirements for running Windows for Workgroups (see "Requirements for Running Windows for Workgroups" at the beginning of this chapter).

✦ Verify that your network interface card is correctly configured and installed (see "Your Network Hardware Does Not Work" earlier in this troubleshooting section).

◆ Verify that the settings for your adapter in the Control Panel's Network option are correct. (See the instructions for viewing and modifying these settings in "Your Network Hardware Does Not Work.")

◆ Verify that the cabling, hubs, and terminators for your LAN are all properly connected.

◆ Watch for error messages on your screen as you boot up. (See "Your Network Hardware Does Not Work" for details.)

You Forget Your Password

If you forget your password, the only way to log on under your present user name is to first delete your password file, then create a new one the first time you log on. You can log on under a new name at any time, but your old password list will be unavailable.

To delete your old password file and create a new one, do the following:

1. View the SYSTEM.INI file using the TYPE and MORE commands or a text editor. Look for the [Password Lists] section, and find the filename that starts with your user name and has a .PWL extension.

2. Delete that password file from your Windows for Workgroups directory.

3. The first time you log in after deleting your password list file, you will be given the opportunity to create a new password list. Choose Yes to create the file.

No Other Computers Appear in Your Connect Dialog Box

If you choose Connect Network Drive from the File Manager's Disk menu, or Connect Network Printer from the Print Manager's Printer menu, you should see a list of the computers in your workgroup. If your own computer is the only one that appears in the Show Shared Directories or the Show Shared Printers lists, try the following:

◆ Make sure that your computer is using the same protocol as the other computers in your workgroup. To find out which protocol you are using, do the following:

Installing and Configuring Windows for Workgroups

1. Double-click on the Network icon in the Control Panel.
2. Click on the Adapters button in the Network Settings dialog box.
3. Click on the Setup button in the Adapter Settings dialog box.
4. Click on the Protocols button. Your protocol is listed in the Protocols In Use box.
5. Click on OK or Close until you are back out to the Control Panel and then double-click on the Control menu box to leave the Control Panel.

✦ Verify that the settings in your PROTOCOL.INI file are the correct ones for your network configuration and are similar to other computers on the network. The only differences among the computers in a network should be due to the differences in the computers themselves; for example, differences in the network cards.

✦ Try waiting for a few minutes (up to five minutes), then try again. This is sometimes necessary when a computer on the LAN is turned off or restarted.

A Particular Computer Does Not Appear on the Network

If you do not see the name of one particular computer in the lists discussed in the preceding section, try the following:

✦ Wait for a few minutes and try again. The computer may have been restarted.

✦ If the computer is part of a workgroup other than your own, you must select or type the workgroup name in the Connect dialog box before the computers in the workgroup appear.

You Are Unable to Share CD-ROM Drive Directories

In order to share directories on a CD-ROM drive with Microsoft CD-ROM Extensions, you must load the MSCDEX.EXE version 2.21 device driver with a command in your AUTOEXEC.BAT file, adding the /S switch.

Problems with Your Mouse

If your mouse does not work properly with Windows for Workgroups, there are several possible solutions:

Check Serial Mouse Port   Make sure that your serial mouse is using either COM1 or COM2. Windows for Workgroups does not support a mouse on COM3 or COM4.

Check for Hardware Interrupt Conflicts   Check for conflicts with the hardware interrupt request line (IRQ) used by your mouse. No other device should use the same IRQ. (See Chapter 3 for information on IRQs and determining which IRQ is used by your mouse. Also see "Your Network Hardware Does Not Work" in this chapter.)

Be Sure Windows Setup Lists Your Mouse   In the Program Manager's Main group, choose Windows Setup, and verify that the type of mouse that you are using appears in the list.

Clean Your Mouse   Your mouse might need to be cleaned. Look for instructions in your mouse documentation.

Using Your Mouse in a Non-Windows Application   If you have problems using your mouse with a non-Windows application running in a window (rather than running full-screen), one of the following might be the cause:

✦ The mouse driver might not have been loaded prior to starting Windows for Workgroups. If you have a Microsoft (or compatible) mouse, use either MOUSE.SYS (loaded in CONFIG.SYS) or MOUSE.COM (loaded in AUTOEXEC.BAT). These files can be copied from your Windows for Workgroups floppy disks (look on Disk 5 or 6) using the EXPAND command, if they are not already in your Windows directory. See the following section, "Copying a File from a Windows Setup Disk."

✦ Your DOS mouse driver might not support the use of a mouse pointer in a windowed DOS application (the Microsoft mouse drivers MOUSE.SYS and MOUSE.COM do). Contact your dealer or the manufacturer of your mouse for an updated driver.

Installing and Configuring Windows for Workgroups

✦ Your display driver might not support the use of a mouse pointer in a windowed DOS application. There might be an updated driver provided by Windows for Workgroups for your display, or you might have to contact the manufacturer of your display adapter for an updated driver. Updated drivers can be installed using the Setup program (located in the \WINDOWS directory), even after Windows for Workgroups is installed.

Copying a File from a Windows Setup Disk

Most of the files on your Windows for Workgroups Setup disks are in compressed form, which minimizes the number of disks required. Any file whose extension ends with an underscore character (_) is compressed and must be expanded before it is usable. Setup automatically expands compressed files as it copies them to your hard disk. If you need to copy a compressed file manually, use the EXPAND.EXE program. EXPAND is located in your Windows directory and is used in the following way:

1. Insert into a floppy drive the disk containing the file(s) that you want to expand. Any file to be expanded must have an underscore at the end of its filename extension.

2. Type the EXPAND command on the DOS command line, as follows:

   expand *sourcefile destinationfile*

   where *sourcefile* is the drive and filename of the compressed file, and *destinationfile* is the drive, directory, and filename of the decompressed file.

3. Rename the compressed file in order to restore the file's original filename extension (without the underscore). The easiest way is to include both the compressed form and the expanded form of the file's name in the EXPAND command. For example, to copy and expand FILENAME.EX_ from drive A to C:\WINDOWS, while restoring its expanded name, FILENAME.EXE, type

   expand a:\filename.ex_ c:\windows\filename.exe

You can expand several files at once by including the name of each in the EXPAND command (no wildcards permitted), but you can only specify the destination drive and directory (not the new filenames). This means that you will have to use the RENAME command later to change the names of the expanded files. For example, to expand the files FILE1.EX_ and FILE2.EX_ on drive A and copy them to the C:\WINDOWS directory, type

expand a:\file1.ex_ a:\file2.ex_ c:\windows

Now you must rename the expanded files so that the .EX_ becomes .EXE. Do this by typing the following:

ren *.ex_ *.exe

For Further Help

If you didn't find a solution to your problem in the preceding topics, you might be able to obtain help in the following ways:

✦ Look for an answer to your problem in the documentation for your hardware or the Windows for Workgroups software.

✦ Browse through online Help, searching for topics related to your problem.

✦ Read the README.WRI file by double-clicking on the ReadMe icon in the Program Manager's Main group. If you cannot use Windows for Workgroups, you can read this file with the DOS Editor, your word processor, or by typing **more < readme.wri**.

✦ Contact Microsoft Product Support Services. They offer a free automated service, FastTips, or for personal assistance, you can call and talk with a member of the staff.

FastTips is a free automated service that gives you recorded messages about Windows for Workgroups. It answers typical questions, offers configuring help for network interface cards, and provides technical notes by fax or mail. Call 206-635-7245 from a touch-tone phone 24 hours a day, including weekends and holidays.

Installing and Configuring Windows for Workgroups

Microsoft Product Support Staff gives you personal assistance in solving your problem. After you have gathered as much information about your problem as you can, and while you are sitting at your computer, call 206-637-7098 (Monday through Friday, 6 a.m. to 6 p.m. Pacific time).

CHAPTER

5 SHARING YOUR RESOURCES WITH THE WORKGROUP

The ability to share your computer's resources is probably one of the major reasons for establishing your Windows for Workgroups network in the first place. Windows for Workgroups makes sharing your computer's files and printers easy, with its enhanced File Manager and Print Manager. Also, the ClipBook Viewer provides an easy way to share information that you have cut or copied from your documents.

Networking Windows for Workgroups

This chapter covers all facets of sharing your resources, including the part played by the File Manager, Print Manager, and ClipBook Viewer. First the concept of sharing your resources is briefly reviewed, then the shared resource path is defined, and finally the steps involved in sharing the various types of resources are covered.

What Does Sharing Your Resources Mean?

In Windows for Workgroups, a *resource* can be a device connected to a computer (a printer or plotter for example), a disk directory and the files stored in it, or information that has been stored in your ClipBook (the ClipBook is a new feature in Windows for Workgroups and is discussed later in this chapter).

If your computer is able to run in 386 enhanced mode you can choose to *share* one or more of the resources on or connected to your computer. (See Chapter 4 for information on the minimum hardware and software requirements for sharing resources.) Others in your workgroup can use the resources that you share in the same way that they use their own computer's resources.

When you share a resource on your computer, you can control who has access to it by assigning passwords to the shared resource. If a password is assigned to a shared resource, only those persons who know the password can use the resource. A shared disk directory or ClipBook page can have a different password assigned to each of two levels of access: read-only or full. *Read-only access* means that users can view files or run applications but cannot make changes to the shared files. *Full access* means that users can run applications, and they can create, change, delete, rename, and move, as well as view files.

REMEMBER: You must be running Windows for Workgroups in 386 enhanced mode before you can share any of your computer's resources.

Sharing Your Resources with the Workgroup

Shared Directory and Printer Paths

The location of a file on a disk is specified by its pathname. The complete *pathname* of a file starts with the drive letter followed by a colon (:) and a backslash (\), which designates the *root* (lowest level) directory of the disk. If the file is not located in the disk's root directory, the names of the directories and subdirectories that must be traversed to get to the file are added, separated by backslashes. Finally, the filename is added at the end, preceded by a backslash. For example, the typical path for the Windows for Workgroups program file is

    C:\WINDOWS\WIN.COM

which specifies that the WIN.COM file is located in the WINDOWS directory on drive C.

When you share a directory on your disk with other workgroup members, the path that they use to refer to your directory is different than the path you use. Your computer has a network name, and you give your directory a name when you share it. (See "Sharing a Disk Directory," later in this chapter, for details.) The network path for your shared files consists of your computer's name preceded by two backslashes (\\), the shared directory's name preceded by one backslash, and finally the filename preceded by one backslash. For example, the network path for a file named RPT.1 located in the shared directory named REPORTS on the computer named BRUCE is

    \\BRUCE\REPORTS\RPT.1

A network printer's path similarly consists of the name of the computer to which it is physically connected (preceded by two backslashes), and the printer's share name preceded by one backslash. For example, the path of a printer with the share name PLOTTER, connected to the computer named BRUCE is

    \\BRUCE\PLOTTER

Networking Windows for Workgroups

Sharing Directories and Closing Files with File Manager

The File Manager (located in the Program Manager's Main group) is the primary Windows for Workgroups tool for performing disk and file management tasks. The File Manager's Share As command is used to share the directories on your disks, and it is covered next.

Sharing a Disk Directory

To designate a directory on your disk as shared, complete the following steps:

1. Double-click on the File Manager icon (the file cabinet) in the Main group. The File Manager window opens, with one or more directory windows open within it (unless you left them minimized the last time you used the File Manager). Figure 5-1 shows the directory window for the CORELDRW\DRAW directory on drive C. The C:\CORELDRW\DRAW directory is not currently shared, as indicated by the words "Not shared" in the status bar at the bottom.

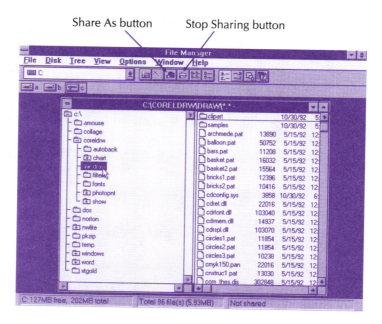

C:\CORELDRW\DRAW directory window in the File Manager
Figure 5-1.

Sharing Your Resources with the Workgroup

2. Select (click on) the icon of the directory that you want to share in the directory tree on the left (if you don't see the tree in your directory window, choose Tree and Directory from the View menu). You can share any directory or subdirectory on any of your disks. Subdirectories are shown in the directory contents list on the right (unless you have selected Tree Only in the View menu), and they can be selected by clicking on their directory icons.

3. When the directory that you want to share is selected, click on the Share As button on the toolbar (the Share As button icon is a hand holding a file folder) or choose Share As from the Disk menu. The Share Directory dialog box appears, as shown here:

The options in the Share Directory dialog box are as follows:

◆ **Share Name** This is the name that you want to give to this shared directory. The share name can be the same as that of the directory, or any other name that describes its contents, and is seen when others browse or connect to shared directories. The Share Name can have up to 12 characters, including letters, numbers, and the following characters:

!   @   # $ %   ^   &   (   )   _   -   .   {   }   '   ~

If you don't want the shared directory to show up when others are browsing your shared directories, end the shared name with a dollar sign ($).

◆ **Path** This is the directory's DOS path, as shown in the directory window's title bar. If you want to share a different directory, you can type its path in this text box.

◆ **Comment** This is an optional description of the shared directory; it appears beside the share name when others browse your shared directories.

◆ **Re-share at Startup** This specifies whether you want this directory to be automatically shared each time you start Windows for Workgroups. Clear this check box if you only want to share the directory during the current session.

◆ **Access Type** This area contains three option buttons:

> ◆ **Read-Only** This specifies that the files in this directory can be viewed and applications can be run, but the files cannot be altered in any way. No files can be deleted from or added to a read-only directory. When this button is selected, a Read-Only password can be assigned to this directory.

> ◆ **Full** This specifies that any of the normal file operations can be performed in this directory, including viewing, editing, deleting, renaming, moving, and adding files, and running application files. When this button is selected, a Full Access password can be assigned to the directory.

> ◆ **Depends on Password** This specifies that users of this directory can have either read-only or full access, depending on which password they have been given. The passwords for the two levels of access are created in the Passwords section of the Share Directory dialog box.

> If you want to allow all of your workgroup members to view files in your shared directory but restrict editing to certain persons, you can designate the directory access as Depends on Password; then type a password for Full Access but leave the Read-Only Password blank.

Sharing Your Resources with the Workgroup

◆ **Passwords** This section contains text boxes in which you type passwords for the two levels of directory access. A directory password can be any combination of eight or fewer characters (numbers and upper- and lowercase letters).

　◆ **Read-Only Password** When Read-Only or Depends on Password access is specified for your shared directory, you can control who has read-only access to it by typing a password in the Read-Only Password text box. If you do not specify a password for a read-only directory, everyone on the LAN is able to view files and run applications in the directory.

　◆ **Full Access Password** When Full or Depends on Password access is specified for your shared directory, you can type a password in the Full Access Password text box to control who has full access to the directory. If you don't type a password here, everyone on the LAN has full access to your directory.

4. Choose the Help button if you need online help with sharing your directories, and choose OK to complete the directory sharing process.

Displaying Users and Closing Files

You can use the File Manager to find out who is using files in your shared directories, and close the shared files if necessary. When someone is using a file it is considered *open*. In some cases you cannot use the file yourself until it has first been closed. If someone has left a file open it might be necessary to force the File Manager to close it, even though it could result in loss of data for the person who opened it.

NOTE: You can also use the Net Watcher application in the Accessories group to display the names of people using your shared directories. (See Chapter 8 for information about the Net Watcher.)

Displaying the Users of a Directory or File

To see a list of the current users of a shared directory or file, follow these steps:

1. In a directory window, select either a shared directory or a file in a shared directory.
2. Choose Properties from the File Manager's File menu, or press [Alt]-[Enter].
3. In the Properties dialog box, choose the Open By button. A dialog box opens, showing either the open files in the selected directory or the people using the selected file, depending on your selection in step 1.

If you selected a *directory* in step 1, the Open Files dialog box appears, as shown here:

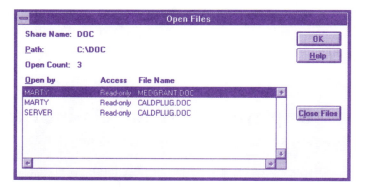

The various elements in the Open Files dialog box are as follows:

✦ **Share Name** This is the name that you gave to the shared directory.

✦ **Path** This is the complete DOS path of the directory, including the drive letter.

✦ **Open Count** This shows the total number of users that have files open in the shared directory. Some files can be used by more than

Sharing Your Resources with the Workgroup

one user at a time, so this figure might exceed the number of files in the directory.

+ **Open by** This column in the list box shows the name of the user who has the file open.

+ **Access** This column shows the type of access (read-only or full) that the user has to the shared directory.

+ **File Name** This column shows the name of the open file.

If you selected a *file* in step 1, the Network Properties dialog box appears, as shown here:

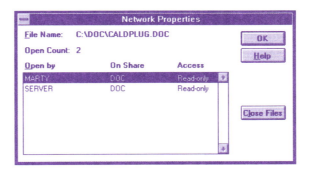

The various elements in the Network Properties dialog box are as follows:

+ **File Name** This is the file that you selected in the directory window.

+ **Open Count** This shows the number of users that have the selected file open.

+ **Open by** This column in the list box shows the name of the user who has the file open.

+ **On Share** This column shows the share name of the directory in which the file is located.

+ **Access** This column shows the type of access (read-only or full) that the user has to the file.

Closing Files

You can close selected files to all users from the Open Files dialog box, or close a selected file to a particular user from the Network Properties dialog box. These two dialog boxes, shown earlier, both contain the Close Files button, which is used to close files.

To close files in the Open Files dialog box, select the files in the list box that you want to close—select as many as you want. Choose the Close Files button to close the selected files to all users on the LAN. The dialog box shown next appears, asking you to confirm that you really want to close these files.

Choose the OK button to close the file, or Cancel to leave it open.

To close files in the Network Properties dialog box, select the particular users for whom you want to close the shared file (you can select multiple users if you want), then choose the Close Files button. Again, you are asked to confirm the action.

CAUTION: If you close a file on a user, the person might lose data. It is safest to notify users before you close files on them.

Changing Access to Your Shared Directories

If you decide that someone to whom you gave your shared directory's password should no longer have access to it, or the person should have read-only instead of full access, you can change one or both of the passwords for the directory. If you do so, however, *nobody* will be able to use their old password(s) for access to the directory. You will have to distribute the new password(s) before the directory can be used by others. This could be disruptive to other workgroup members and

Sharing Your Resources with the Workgroup

time-consuming for you, so plan this action carefully and perform it at a non-critical time, if possible.

You can also stop sharing a directory altogether. After you stop sharing a directory, it no longer appears when others browse your shared directories. To stop sharing a directory, follow these steps:

1. In the directory window select the icon of the shared directory that you want to stop sharing.
2. Choose the Stop Sharing button on the File Manager's toolbar or choose Stop Sharing on the Disk menu. The Stop Sharing Directory dialog box appears, as shown here:

3. Select one or more directories from the list of shared directories that you want to stop sharing and then choose the OK button. If others are using files in a directory that you want to stop sharing, a warning message appears.

CAUTION: If you stop sharing a directory while others are connected to it they might lose data. Before using the Stop Sharing option, find out who is connected to the directory (see "Displaying Users and Closing Files" earlier in this chapter), and notify them that you want to stop sharing the directory.

Using the Print Manager to Share a Printer

The Print Manager application is used for many printer-related tasks, including setting up both local and network printers, choosing a default printer, managing print jobs, connecting to network printers, and sharing your printer with others.

Networking Windows for Workgroups

This section discusses the Print Manager features that enable you to share your printer (or other connected device) with other members of your workgroup.

REMEMBER: Your computer must be running in 386 enhanced mode in order to share its resources.

Designating a Printer as Shared

You can designate as shared any printer that is directly connected to your computer. The printer must first be set up on your computer, which is normally done for you when you run the Windows for Workgroups Setup program. To share a printer that has been set up on your computer, do the following:

1. Choose the Print Manager icon in the Main group. The Print Manager window opens, as shown in Figure 5-2.
2. In the list of printers, select the printer that you want to share. Notice in Figure 5-2 that the words "not shared" appear after the printer names.

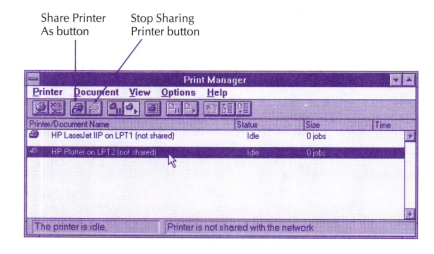

Print Manager window prior to sharing
Figure 5-2.

Sharing Your Resources with the Workgroup

3. Choose the Share Printer As button on the toolbar (the button that shows a hand holding a printer), or choose Share Printer As from the Printer menu. The Share Printer dialog box appears, as shown here:

The Share Printer dialog box contains the following options:

✦ **Printer** This shows the printer (and its port) that you selected in the Print Manager window. If you want to share a different printer, click on the down arrow at the right, then select the printer from the Printer list.

✦ **Share as** This is the name that you want to give to this shared printer. This name is seen when others browse or connect to shared printers. If you want to use a name other than the one shown, type the name in this text box, using up to 12 characters, including letters, numbers, and the following characters:

! @ # $ % ^ & ( ) _ - . { } ' ~

If you don't want the shared printer to show up when others are browsing your shared printers in the Connect Network Printer dialog box (covered in Chapter 6), end the shared name with a dollar sign ($).

✦ **Comment** This is a description of your shared printer or any other instructions or notes that you want to appear beside the share name when others browse your shared printers. The comment is optional and can contain up to 48 characters.

✦ **Password** This enables you to control who can use your printer. If you do not type a password in this text box everyone on the LAN is able to send print jobs to your printer. A password can be any combination of eight or fewer characters (numbers and upper- and lowercase letters).

✦ **Re-share at Startup** This specifies whether you want this printer to be automatically shared each time you start Windows for Workgroups. Clear this check box if you only want to share the printer during the current session.

The Share Printer dialog box shown earlier has been completed in the following illustration:

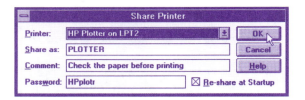

4. Choose the Help button if you need online help with sharing your printer, and choose OK to complete the sharing process. After the HP Plotter has been designated as shared, with the name PLOTTER, the Print Manager window looks like this:

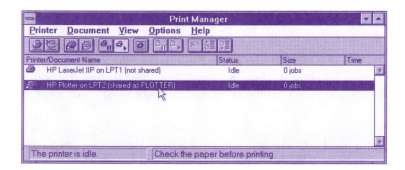

Notice that the words "shared as PLOTTER" now appear after the printer's name, and that its icon is a hand holding a printer. In addition, the optional comment appears in the status bar at the bottom of the window.

Viewing and Canceling Document Printing

Under the name of each printer in the Print Manager window is a list of the documents (if any) currently waiting to be printed on the printer. These include your own and others' documents.

NOTE: You can also use the Net Watcher application in the Accessories group to display the names of people using your shared printer. (See Chapter 8 for more information about the Net Watcher application.)

You can cancel the printing of any document on your *local* printer (one that is directly connected to your computer) by deleting the document from the list of documents.

From the list of documents waiting to be printed on a *network* printer (not directly connected to your computer) you can only delete your own documents, and only if they have not yet started to print.

To delete a document from the Print Manager's list of documents waiting to be printed, follow these steps:

1. In the Print Manager window, select the document that you want to delete.
2. Click on the Delete Document button on the toolbar (third from the right), choose Delete Document from the Document menu, or press (Del).

You can also cancel the printing of all documents on your local printer(s) by exiting Print Manager. This can be accomplished by pressing (Alt)-(F4) or choosing Exit from the Printer menu while the Print Manager window is your active window. If the Print Manager is running as an icon on your desktop, you can quit it by clicking on its icon and then choosing Close from its Control menu. When you use any of these methods to quit the Print Manager and you have designated your printer as shared, the following warning message appears:

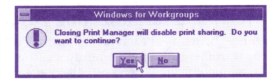

If you wish to temporarily disable the sharing of your printer and cancel all printing, choose Yes. The next time you start your computer, the Print Manager will automatically be started if you have any of your local printers designated as shared.

Changing Access to Your Shared Printer

If you decide that someone to whom you gave your shared printer's password should no longer have access to it, you can change the password for the printer. This is accomplished by typing a new password in the Share Printer dialog box (follow the directions in "Designating a Printer as Shared" earlier in this chapter). As with changing a password for a shared directory, you will have to notify all those to whom you have given your shared printer's password of the change.

You can also stop sharing your printer altogether. After you stop sharing a printer, it no longer appears when others browse or connect to shared printers. To stop sharing your printer, follow these steps:

1. In the Print Manager's list of printers, select the printer that you want to stop sharing (the printer's icon is a hand holding a printer if it is shared).

2. Choose the Stop Sharing Printer button on the Print Manager's toolbar (fourth from the left) or choose Stop Sharing Printer on the Disk menu. The Stop Sharing Printer dialog box appears, as shown here:

Sharing Your Resources with the Workgroup

3. Select the printer(s) to stop sharing, then click on OK.

Using the ClipBook Viewer to Share Local ClipBook Pages

Each computer on a Windows for Workgroups network has a Local ClipBook. Your Local ClipBook is a permanent place to store the information that you cut or copy to your Clipboard. Once the information is in your Local ClipBook it can be shared with others on the network. The ClipBook Viewer is used to transfer information between the Clipboard and the Local ClipBook, to connect to the ClipBooks of others on the network, and to share your Local ClipBook pages.

First, the ways of getting information onto the Clipboard are briefly discussed, then the sharing of that information is covered.

Moving Information onto the Clipboard

The methods you use for getting information from your application onto the Clipboard depend on whether the application is a Windows or a non-Windows application.

Cutting and Copying from Windows Applications

Windows applications typically have an Edit menu with commands for cutting and copying onto the Clipboard. Here's how to use these tools:

1. In a Windows application, select the text or graphics that you want to copy.
2. From the Edit menu, choose either Cut (to remove the information and place it onto the Clipboard) or Copy (to leave the original information while placing a copy onto the Clipboard).

You can also copy the entire desktop (screen) onto the Clipboard by pressing Prt Sc.

In 386 enhanced mode, you can copy the contents of just the active window by pressing Alt-Prt Sc.

Copying From Non-Windows Applications

When you are running a non-Windows application in full-screen mode you can copy the entire screen to the Clipboard in the same way that you copy the entire desktop to the Clipboard: by pressing [Prt Sc].

When running a non-Windows application in 386 enhanced mode, you can copy selected information to the Clipboard with the following steps:

1. While in your non-Windows application running full screen, press [Alt]-[Enter] to run the application in a window.
2. Click on the Control menu box or press [Alt]-[Spacebar] to open the Control menu, then choose Edit.
3. Choose Mark from the Edit menu.
4. Select the information in your application that you want to copy to the Clipboard.
5. Press the right mouse button or press [Enter] to complete the copy.

Pasting the Clipboard Contents into Your Local ClipBook

Once the information that you want to share is on the Clipboard, you can save it to your Local ClipBook and share it as follows:

1. Double-click on the ClipBook Viewer icon in the Main group. The ClipBook Viewer window opens, with document windows (or sub-windows) for the Clipboard and the Local ClipBook.

   Figure 5-3 shows an example ClipBook Viewer window with the Clipboard and Local ClipBook windows open, and some copied text (from the Write document NETWORKS.WRI) in the Clipboard window.

2. Select the Local ClipBook window (click anywhere in it or choose it from the Window menu).

3. Click on the Paste button (fifth from the right in the toolbar), or choose Paste from the Edit menu, to paste the Clipboard contents

Sharing Your Resources with the Workgroup

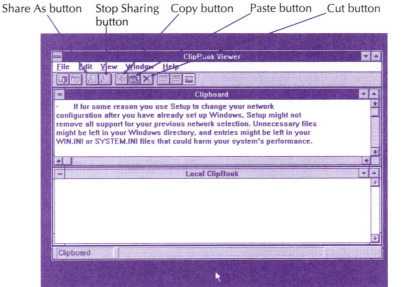

ClipBook Viewer window with Clipboard and ClipBook windows
Figure 5-3.

to a new Local ClipBook page. The dialog box appears, as shown here:

4. Type a descriptive name for the new ClipBook page in the Page Name text box.
5. If you want to share this page, click on the Share Item Now check box to place an X in it.
6. Click on OK. If you checked Share Item Now, the Share ClipBook Page dialog box appears, as shown in Figure 5-4.

The options in the Share ClipBook Page dialog box are as follows:

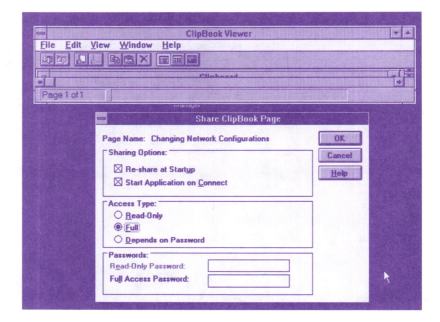

Share ClipBook Page dialog box
Figure 5-4.

✦ **Page Name**   This is the name that you gave the new ClipBook page in the Paste dialog box shown earlier.

✦ **Sharing Options**   This area contains two options:

   ✦ **Re-share at Startup**   This specifies whether you want this ClipBook page to be automatically shared each time you start Windows for Workgroups. Clear this check box if you only want to share this page during the current session.

   ✦ **Start Application on Connect**   This specifies that the application used to create the information on the shared ClipBook page is automatically started when someone connects to your ClipBook. If you don't check this box, others on your network will not be able to establish a link to your ClipBook page information unless the application happens to be running.

✦ **Access Type**   This area contains three option buttons:

Sharing Your Resources with the Workgroup

◆ **Read-Only**   This specifies that the ClipBook page cannot be altered in any way. When this button is selected, a Read-Only password can be assigned to this ClipBook page.

◆ **Full**   This specifies that others can make changes to this ClipBook page. When this button is selected, a Full Access password can be assigned to this ClipBook page.

◆ **Depends on Password**   This specifies that a user of this ClipBook page can have either read-only or full access, depending on which password the user has been given. The passwords for the two levels of access are created in the Passwords section.

◆ **Passwords**   This area contains text boxes for typing passwords for the two levels of ClipBook page access. A password can be any combination of eight or fewer characters (numbers and upper- and lowercase letters).

◆ **Read-Only Password**   When Read-Only or Depends on Password access is specified for your shared ClipBook page, you can control who has read-only access to it by typing a password in the Read-Only Password text box. If you do not specify a password here, everyone on the LAN is able to view the ClipBook page.

◆ **Full Access Password**   When Full or Depends on Password access is specified for your shared ClipBook page, you can control who has full access to the page by typing a password in the Full Access Password text box. If you don't type a password here, everyone on the LAN has full access to your ClipBook page.

7. Choose the Help button if you need online help with sharing your ClipBook page, and choose OK to make your ClipBook page shared.

The shared page now appears in the Local ClipBook window, with an icon that looks like a hand holding a notebook. Figure 5-5 shows the shared ClipBook page created from the Clipboard contents shown above it.

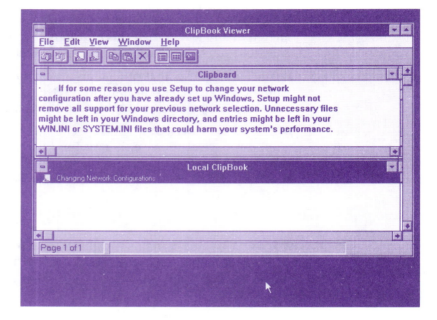

**ClipBook Viewer window with a shared page
Figure 5-5.**

Changing Access to Your Shared ClipBook Page

As with a shared directory, if you decide that someone to whom you gave a password for access to your shared ClipBook page should no longer have access to it, or should have read-only instead of full access, you can change one or both of the passwords for the shared page. Again, you will have to distribute the new password(s) before the ClipBook page can be used by others who have the old password(s).

You can also stop sharing a ClipBook page altogether. After you stop sharing a ClipBook page, it no longer appears when others browse your shared pages. To stop sharing a Local ClipBook page, follow these steps:

1. Select the page that you want to stop sharing in the Local ClipBook window.
2. Choose the Stop Sharing button on the ClipBook Viewer's toolbar or choose Stop Sharing on the File menu. The icon for the ClipBook page changes to a notebook without the hand.

Sharing Your Resources with the Workgroup

Stopping the Sharing of All Your Resources

You can stop sharing all disk directories, printers, and ClipBook pages in one operation, if you want. This is accomplished as follows:

1. Double-click on the Control Panel icon in the Program Manager's Main group.
2. In the Control Panel window, choose the Network icon.
3. In the Network Settings dialog box, clear (remove the check mark from) the Enable Sharing check box. (See "Customizing Network Settings" in Chapter 4 for more information on the Network Settings dialog box.)

CHAPTER

6 CONNECTING TO THE WORKGROUP RESOURCES

Once other members of your workgroup have made one or more of their computer's resources available to you by sharing *them (which is covered in Chapter 5), you* can connect *to those resources in order to use them. Unlike sharing resources, which requires that your computer run in 386 enhanced mode, connecting to and using shared resources can be accomplished in either standard or 386 enhanced* mode. This means that the more powerful 386 and 486 computers on your Windows for Workgroups network can share their resources with the less powerful 286 computers. This arrangement is similar to the client-server type of networks discussed in Chapter 1. If your network consists entirely of 386 and newer computers, then every computer can share its resources with the others, resulting in a true peer-to-peer network.

This chapter covers using the File Manager, Print Manager, and ClipBook Viewer to connect to shared resources on your network. You connect to shared disk directories with File Manager, to shared printers with Print Manager, and to ClipBook pages that others have designated as shared with the ClipBook Viewer.

Using Shared Directories

When you connect to a shared directory on another computer, you assign an unused drive letter to it. This results in the creation of a new *network drive* that you can use in both Windows and DOS just like you use the drives located on your own computer. The root directory of the network drive is the shared directory, and includes the shared directory's subdirectories, if any.

Reserving Drive Letters with the LASTDRIVE Command

Your system uses the first few letters of the alphabet (typically A through C or D) as drive letters for your own disk drives. The LASTDRIVE command specifies the highest drive letter that is reserved for assigning to the other drives on your network. The LASTDRIVE command is placed in your CONFIG.SYS file, and it usually reserves the maximum possible number of drive letters, for example:

```
LASTDRIVE=Z
```

You can save a little memory (about 100 bytes per letter) by reserving only the number of drive letters that you will actually use, rather than all the letters from A to Z. If you find, for example, that you never use more than eight shared directories and you use the letters A, B, and C

Connecting to the Workgroup Resources

for your own drives, you can specify the letter K in the LASTDRIVE command, for example:

LASTDRIVE=K

Browsing and Connecting to a Shared Directory

The File Manager enables you to browse through a list of all the shared directories on your Windows for Workgroups network and connect to any of them in order to use the files stored there. To view the shared directories available and connect to one or more, follow these steps:

1. Start the File Manager by choosing (double-clicking on) its icon in the Main group. The File Manager window opens, with one or more directory windows contained within it. Figure 6-1 shows the directory window for the CD3\DRAW directory on drive C. (See "Shared Directory and Printer Paths" in Chapter 5 for a brief discussion of directory paths and pathnames.)

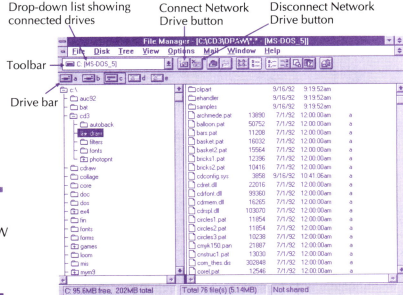

File Manager with the C:\CD3\DRAW directory window
Figure 6-1.

2. Click on the Connect Network Drive button in the toolbar, or choose Connect Network Drive from the Disk menu. The Connect Network Drive dialog box appears, as shown in Figure 6-2.

3. Specify the drive letter and shared directory path for your network drive in this dialog box.

The Connect Network Drive dialog box has the following features:

✦ **Drive** This text box initially contains the next available drive letter not assigned to a local drive or a shared network directory. If you want to use a different letter, click on the down arrow at the right of the Drive box to get a list of drive letters, as shown here:

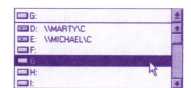

The Connect Network Drive dialog box appears when you click on the Connect button
Figure 6-2.

Connecting to the Workgroup Resources

Select the drive letter that you want to use for your new network drive (notice that any previous connections also appear on this list). The list closes, and the letter you chose now appears in the Drive box.

✦ **Path** The path of the shared directory that you are connecting to must be specified in this text box. As discussed in "Shared Directory and Printer Paths" in Chapter 5, the path of a network directory consists of the computer name followed by the shared name given to it when it is designated as shared.

There are three ways to specify the path: you can either type the directory's path in the Path box (in the form *computername* *sharename*), click on the down arrow at the right to select from a list of previously used directory paths, or browse through and select a directory from the Shared Directories list box at the bottom of the dialog box.

✦ **Show Shared Directories on** To browse through the connected computers on a workgroup, first expand a workgroup in the Show Shared Directories on list box by double-clicking on the workgroup icon. A list of the workgroup's member computers appears, with comments beside those users who entered one. (See "Customizing Network Settings" in Chapter 4 for instructions on adding a comment next to your computer's name.) When you select a computer from this list, the shared directories on that computer appear in the Shared Directories list box at the bottom of the dialog box, and the computer name appears in the Path box near the top of the dialog box.

Figure 6-3 shows the Connect Network Drive dialog box after the workgroup has been expanded and a computer selected.

✦ **Shared Directories** After browsing through and selecting a computer name in the Show Shared Directories on area, all the shared directories on the selected computer appear in the Shared Directories list box (unless they were given a shared name ending with a dollar sign). The comment (if any) that is created when sharing a directory appears here, next to the shared name. (See "Sharing a Disk Directory" in Chapter 5 for instructions on creating

Connect Network Drive dialog box after a workgroup computer has been selected in the Show Shared Directories on area
Figure 6-3.

a comment for a shared directory.) Select (click on) a shared directory to add its name after the computer's name in the Path box.

REMEMBER: Directory names, filenames, and printer names ending in a dollar sign do not appear as shared directories even though they actually are.

◆ **Reconnect at Startup** Clear this check box if you don't want to automatically connect to this shared directory each time you start Windows for Workgroups.

4. Click on the Help button if you want to see the online help for the Connect Network Drive dialog box, and click on the OK button to complete the creation of your new network drive. If a password is

Connecting to the Workgroup Resources

required for access to the shared directory the Enter Network Password dialog box appears, as shown here:

Enter the password given to you by the person sharing this directory. If the directory has two access levels, the password you type here determines which level of access you get to the files on the directory. If the check box next to Save this Password in Your Password List is checked, you will not have to type the password the next time you connect to this directory.

A new directory window for the network drive you just created automatically appears if the Open New Window on Connect option in the File Manager's Options menu is checked. In addition, an icon for the new network drive appears in the File Manager's drive bar (see Figure 6-1), and the drive is added to the drop-down list of drives on the toolbar.

Disconnecting from a Shared Directory

Disconnecting from a network drive is as simple as clicking on a button. Try that next with these steps:

1. Click on the Disconnect Network Drive button in the File Manager's toolbar, or choose Disconnect Network Drive from the Disk menu. A list of the network drives to which you are connected appears.
2. Select one or more drives, then click on the OK button.

Using Shared Printers

When you connect to a shared printer that is physically connected to someone else's computer (a network printer), you assign a parallel (LPT) port number to it much like you assign a drive letter to a shared directory. The port number that you assign to a network printer is an arbitrary number, and need not exist as a physical port on either your computer or the computer to which the network printer is connected. Once you connect to a network printer you can use it in the same way that you use a local printer that is connected by a cable to a physical port on your computer.

Connecting to a Network Printer

You use the Print Manager application to connect to a shared printer on your Windows for Workgroups network, in the same way that you use the File Manager to connect to shared directories.

To browse through a list of the available network printers and connect to any of them, follow these steps:

1. Start the Print Manager (if it is not already running) by choosing (double-clicking on) its icon in the Main group. The Print Manager window opens, as shown in Figure 6-4. If the Print Manager is already running, click on it if you can see it on your screen, or

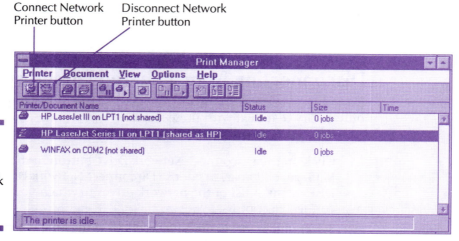

Print Manager window showing a shared network printer
Figure 6-4.

Connecting to the Workgroup Resources

press and hold [Alt] while pressing [Tab] until you see a message that says "Print Manager."

2. Click on the Connect Network Printer button in the Print Manager's toolbar, or choose Connect Network Printer from the Printer menu. The Connect Network Printer dialog box appears, as shown in Figure 6-5.

3. Specify the port and shared printer path for your network printer in this dialog box.

The Connect Network Printer dialog box has the following features:

✦ **Device Name** This text box initially contains a suggested port (LPT) number. If you want to use a different port (remember that the port you select does not have to be a physical port on your computer), first make sure that the Device Name box is highlighted, then type the number or use your up and down arrow keys to increase or decrease the number shown. To see a list of ports, click

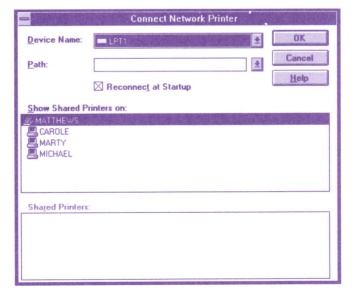

Connect Network Printer dialog box
Figure 6-5.

on the down arrow at the right. A sample Device Name list is shown here:

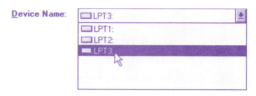

Select the port number that you want to use for your network printer connection. You can select a port number currently in use if you want to replace the existing port assignment. The port that you choose appears in the Device Name box.

✦ **Path** The path of the shared printer that you are connecting to must be specified in the Path text box. As discussed in "Shared Directory and Printer Paths" in Chapter 5, the path of a network printer consists of the computer name followed by the shared name given to it when it is designated as shared.

There are three ways to specify the path: you can either type the path in the Path box (in the form *computername**sharename*), click on the down arrow at the right of the text box to select from a list of previously used printers, or browse through and select a shared printer from the Shared Printers list box at the bottom of the dialog box.

✦ **Show Shared Printers on** To browse through a list of the computers on the network, first expand the workgroup in the Show Shared Printers on list box by double-clicking on the workgroup icon. A list of the workgroup's member computers appears, with comments beside those users who created one. When you select a computer from this list, the shared printers (if any) connected to that computer appear in the Shared Printers list box at the bottom of the dialog box, and the computer's name appears in the Path box near the top of the dialog box.

Figure 6-6 shows the Connect Network Printer dialog box after a workgroup has been expanded and a computer selected.

✦ **Shared Printers on** After browsing through and selecting a computer name in the Show Shared Printers on area, the shared

Connecting to the Workgroup Resources

Connect Network Printer dialog box showing shared printers
Figure 6-6.

printers (if any) connected to the selected computer appear in the Shared Printers on list box (except for those printers whose shared name ends with a dollar sign). If a comment was created when the printer was designated as shared, it appears beside the shared name. Select a shared printer to add its name after the computer's name in the Path box near the top of the dialog box.

♦ **Reconnect at Startup** Clear this check box if you don't want to automatically connect to this network printer each time you start Windows for Workgroups.

4. Click on the Help button if you want to see the online help for the Connect Network Printer dialog box, and click on OK to complete the connection to the network printer.

NOTE: If you have not set up the software for using this network printer before, you will be prompted to do so at this point. See the next section, "Setting Up a Network Printer," for instructions.

If a password is required for access to the network printer, you are prompted to type it. (See the earlier section, "Browsing and Connecting to a Shared Directory," for an example of the dialog box that appears.)

 The network printer that you connected to appears in the Print Manager's window with the Network Printer icon next to it.

Setting Up a Network Printer

Before you can use a network printer you must set it up in the same way that you set up a local printer physically connected to your computer. (Setting up a local printer is usually done when you run Setup to install Windows for Workgroups.) If you try to connect to a network printer that has not been set up on the port you assign it, you are prompted to set it up.

NOTE: The PRINTERS.WRI file provided with Windows for Workgroups contains information about setting up specific printers. It can be viewed using the Write application in the Accessories group.

Set up a shared network printer with the following steps:

1. Choose Printer Setup from the Print Manager's Options menu (or click on the OK button if you have been prompted to set up a printer). The Printers dialog box appears, as shown in Figure 6-7. Click on the Add button if the List of Printers box does not appear in your Printers dialog box.

2. Double-click on the name of your printer in the list, or select it and click on the install button.

If your printer is not listed but emulates one that is listed, choose that one. If your printer uses a PostScript cartridge that emulates a listed printer, choose that printer. If your printer uses a PostScript cartridge that does not emulate a listed printer, choose the PostScript version of your printer if listed, otherwise choose PostScript printer. Choose Generic/Text Only for a daisy-wheel printer, or Install Unlisted or Updated Printer if you have a Windows printer driver on a disk supplied by the printer's manufacturer.

Connecting to the Workgroup Resources

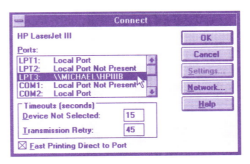

Printers dialog box showing the list of printers
Figure 6-7.

You might be prompted to insert one or more of your Windows for Workgroups floppy disks (or your printer manufacturer's disk if you choose Install Unlisted or Updated Printer). Click on the Help button for assistance with these and other features of the Printers dialog box.

3. Make sure that the network printer is selected in the Installed Printers list near the top of the Printers dialog box, then click on the Connect button. The Connect dialog box, shown below, appears.

4. In the Connect dialog box, select the port that you previously assigned to the shared printer from the Ports list. If it does not appear in this list, click on the Network button to specify a network port and path for the network printer (see "Connecting to a Network Printer," earlier, for instructions). If you need help with

the other printer setup options in the Connect dialog box, click on the Help button.

5. Make sure that the correct network printer and port are highlighted in the Ports list box, then click on OK.

6. Click on the Close button in the Printers dialog box to complete setting up your network printer.

Disconnecting from a Network Printer

Disconnecting from a network printer is similar to disconnecting from a shared directory. Use the following instructions for that purpose:

1. Click on the Disconnect Network Printer button in the Print Manager's toolbar, or choose Disconnect Network Printer from the Printer menu. A list of the network printers to which you are connected appears.

2. Select one or more printers, then click on the OK button.

Using Shared ClipBook Pages

Chapter 5 covered the procedures for sharing pages in your Local ClipBook with other people in your Windows for Workgroups network. In this chapter the process of connecting to and using the information in the shared ClipBook pages is covered.

Introduction to the ClipBook Viewer

Each computer on a Windows for Workgroups network has a Local ClipBook, as well as a Clipboard. The Clipboard is a temporary storage location for selected information that has been cut or copied from your applications, or for an entire window or screen that has been copied. (See Chapter 5 for instructions on transferring information onto the Clipboard.) The Clipboard can hold only one piece of information at a time, so each time you transfer information onto the Clipboard the previous information is replaced. In addition, the contents of the Clipboard are lost when you leave Windows for Workgroups.

Connecting to the Workgroup Resources

Once on the Clipboard, information can be transferred to your Local ClipBook for permanent storage. The information in your Local ClipBook pages can be transferred back onto your Clipboard at any time, and then pasted into your applications. Shared ClipBook pages of others can also be copied onto your Clipboard and used in the same way. In addition, ClipBook pages can be used for object linking and embedding.

The ClipBook Viewer application is used to work with your Clipboard and Local ClipBook, as well as the shared ClipBook pages of others. The ClipBook Viewer is started by choosing (double-clicking on) its icon in the Program Manager's Main group. When you do that, the ClipBook Viewer window opens, as shown in Figure 6-8. The ClipBook Viewer application window contains document windows for the Local ClipBook and the Clipboard (shown minimized in the lower-left corner), as well as for each shared ClipBook to which you have connected.

The buttons located on the toolbar (just below the menu bar) represent almost all of the ClipBook Viewer commands. They are used for the following operations (reading from left to right):

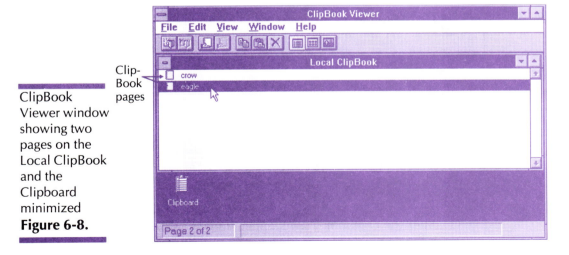

ClipBook Viewer window showing two pages on the Local ClipBook and the Clipboard minimized
Figure 6-8.

Button	Purpose
Connect	Connect to another computer's ClipBook
Disconnect	Disconnect from another computer's ClipBook
Share	Share a ClipBook page
Stop Sharing	Stop sharing a ClipBook page
Copy	Copy a selected page to the Clipboard
Paste	Paste the Clipboard contents to a ClipBook page
Cut	Delete the Clipboard contents or a ClipBook page
Table of Contents	View the ClipBook page titles available
Thumbnails	View thumbnail (tiny) pictures of the ClipBook pages available
Full Page	View the contents of a selected ClipBook page

Connecting to a Shared ClipBook Page

To connect to the shared ClipBook pages of another computer in your Windows for Workgroups network, follow these steps:

1. Start the ClipBook Viewer application by double-clicking on the ClipBook Viewer icon in the Program Manager's Main group. The ClipBook Viewer window opens, as shown in Figure 6-8.

Connecting to the Workgroup Resources

2. Click on the Connect button in the toolbar, or choose Connect from the File menu. The Select Computer dialog box appears, as shown here:

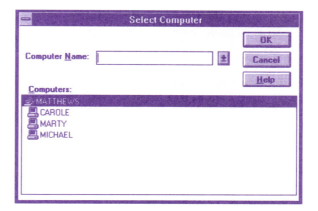

3. Specify the name of the computer whose ClipBook you want to connect to in the Computer Name text box. There are three ways to accomplish this:

    ◆ Type the computer name directly into the Computer Name box, including the double-backslash (\\) at the beginning.

    ◆ Click on the down arrow at the right of the Computer Name box to open a list of the computers to which you have previously connected. Select a name from the list to reconnect to it.

    ◆ In the Computers list box at the bottom, double-click on a workgroup icon to expand the list of its member computers. From the list of computers, select the one to which you want to connect. The computer's name appears in the Computer Name box.

4. When the computer's name appears in the Computer Name box, click on the OK button. A new window in the ClipBook Viewer window appears, with a list of the shared ClipBook pages available on the

computer you selected. Figure 6-9 shows the ClipBook Viewer window after connecting to a network computer's ClipBook.

Disconnecting from a Shared ClipBook

Disconnecting from another workgroup member's ClipBook is as simple as disconnecting from a shared directory or printer. Use these steps:

1. Select (click on) the window of the remote ClipBook from which you want to disconnect.

2. Click on the Disconnect button in the ClipBook Viewer toolbar, or choose Disconnect from the File menu. The remote ClipBook's window closes.

Using the Information on ClipBook Pages

The information stored in both your Local ClipBook pages and the shared ClipBook pages of others can be inserted into your documents in three different ways: by simple pasting, by embedding, and by linking.

ClipBook Viewer window after connecting with the ClipBook on another computer
Figure 6-9.

Connecting to the Workgroup Resources

When information is pasted into your documents, it is simply copied there. There is no connection to the original (*source*) application or document, and there is no ability to edit the information in your document (the *destination*), unless the information was created in the same application as the destination document.

An *embedded object* in your document is a copy of information from the source document. It can be edited within your document simply by double-clicking on the embedded object. The changes made to the embedded object are *not* reflected in the source document. A *linked object* in your document can also be edited simply by double-clicking on it. However, it retains a direct link with the original object, and both are automatically changed when a change is made to either one of them.

An object must have been created in a Windows application that supports *object linking and embedding* (*OLE*) in order for you to use it for embedding or linking. In addition, objects can be embedded or linked only into a Windows application that supports OLE. If either the source or destination application does not support OLE, you can only paste the information into your documents. The methods used for all three ways of using ClipBook pages are similar, but different applications might use slightly different methods. The main points of pasting, linking, and embedding are summarized here:

◆ The object or information that you want to copy, embed, or link must first be transferred (copied) onto your Clipboard, using the source application's or the ClipBook Viewer's Copy command.

◆ If your destination document is in a Windows application, position the pointer where you want to insert the object or information. Then choose Paste from the Edit menu if you want to embed the Clipboard contents into your document. To link or paste the Clipboard contents into your document, choose Paste Special from the Edit menu. Then choose the appropriate option, either Paste Link or Paste.

◆ To paste into a non-Windows application running full screen, position the cursor where you want to insert the Clipboard contents, press [Alt]-[Spacebar] to open the Control menu, and then choose Edit and Paste. (If your application uses [Alt]-[Spacebar] for its own function, press [Ctrl]-[Esc] to minimize the application to an icon, then click on the icon to open its Control menu.)

Consult your applications manuals to determine whether they support object linking and embedding, and what the exact procedures are for these tasks.

CHAPTER

7 USING WINDOWS FOR WORKGROUPS' MAIL

The essence of networking is the ability to communicate—to exchange thoughts and data with other computer users in your workgroup. This chapter introduces Windows for Workgroups' Mail, a system that allows you to send messages and files electronically over your network. Using Mail reduces paper memoranda, and the lost pieces of paper and other inefficiencies associated with the "paper shuffle."

After introducing you to Mail, this chapter leads you through several exercises in the use of electronic mail. The exercises include sending, receiving, and replying to mail; establishing group broadcasts and an address book; attaching files such as word processing or spreadsheet documents to your messages; and forwarding comments among a series of readers.

Introducing Mail

Mail is organized much like a post office. There is a central clearinghouse where mail is organized, sorted, and distributed. In Mail, this is called the *Workgroup Postoffice*. Within a post office there are *accounts*, or mailboxes, for people to receive and send mail. Mail establishes individual accounts for each member of the workgroup. Finally, Mail provides a full help system using the familiar Windows Help facility.

The Workgroup Postoffice

The Workgroup Postoffice defines the set of people who can communicate with one another. In order to use Mail with others in your group, all of you must belong to the same Workgroup Postoffice. One member of the group is assigned the duties of setting up accounts for the other members and attending to the administration of Postoffice files. This account is called the *Postoffice Administration Account.* The first person to set up a Postoffice is its administrator. There is one such account for each Workgroup Postoffice. The actual mechanics of establishing the Workgroup Postoffice and the Postoffice Administration Account are discussed in the section called "The Workgroup Postoffice Administrator," following the exercises on Mail's use.

To illustrate the Workgroup Postoffice concept, Figure 7-1A shows two groups that have formed Postoffices within their respective areas. Both the Accounting Department and the Sales Department are connected to the same network, but each has a separate Postoffice that communicates solely within each department. Members of different Workgroup Postoffices cannot communicate with each other. In order for people in Accounting to send and receive mail with Sales, a new Workgroup

Using Windows for Workgroups' Mail

Postoffice needs to be established that combines the members of the two departments, as shown in Figure 7-1B.

Your Personal Mailbox

Each person has a high degree of freedom in managing his or her own mailbox and outgoing and incoming correspondence. Mail provides you with a default electronic Inbox and Outbox, which list your received and sent messages. Additionally, you can create folders, similar to directories, that allow you to file messages by topic. These folders can then be coded to be shared among other Postoffice users or held private. Figure 7-2 shows the Inbox with an example list of private folders.

Your personal mailbox is unique to you, the user. It provides several convenient and timesaving features; for example, you have your own password to assure confidentiality, a personal address book which allows you to quickly send messages to other members of your Postoffice, and the ability to set up groups of people within your Postoffice who you can address as a group instead of individually.

Mail Help

Mail Help uses the standard Windows Help facility you learned about in Chapter 2. If you press [F1] and choose the Contents option from the Help menu, or click on the Help button in many dialog boxes, the Mail Help Contents window appears, as shown in Figure 7-3.

Figure 7-1. Examples of isolated workgroups (*A*) and communicating workgroups (*B*)

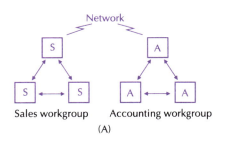
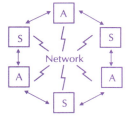

Networking Windows for Workgroups

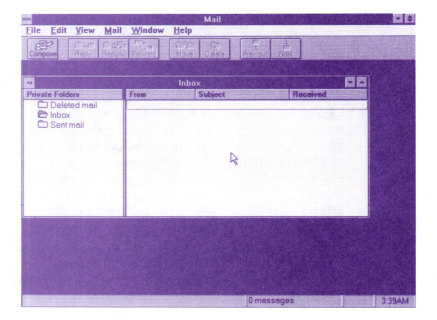

Mail's Inbox containing a list of private folders
Figure 7-2.

Mail Help contents
Figure 7-3.

The major topics of Mail Help are listed in the opening window. The topics that have a + sign in the command button before their names have additional subtopics. You access these subtopics by clicking on the command button with the mouse pointer or by using the [Tab] key to select the topic and then press [Enter]. Alternatively, you can view the topics and all of their subtopics on the screen by choosing the Expand button under the title.

Each subtopic (or the two topics without subtopics) provides information and, often, step-by-step procedures on how to perform a task. Also, each subtopic screen contains an Overview button that offers a brief synopsis. Finally, underlined keywords and related topics and subtopics can be chosen to further enhance your knowledge on a specific subject. For example, choose the Using the Address Book topic, then the Updating Your Personal Address Book subtopic. Click on the Overview button to display the following:

In the next several sections, you will perform a number of exercises using Mail. Now is a good time to turn on your computer, if it isn't already, and have the Windows Program Manager on your screen.

Getting Started

Depending on your network situation, your first use of Mail can take two different paths:

✦ Connect to an existing Workgroup Postoffice that someone has already established.

✦ Create a Workgroup Postoffice and become the administrator.

The exercises that follow relate to the first path. If you need to create a Postoffice (the second path), refer to the section titled, "The Workgroup Postoffice Administrator," later in this chapter.

Starting Mail for the First Time

With the Program Manager window on your screen, use the following instructions to start Mail.

1. Open the Main group. The Main group window appears on your screen. Windows 3.1 users will notice the addition of two icons, Mail and Schedule+, and a change from the Clipboard Viewer to the ClipBook Viewer.

2. Double-click on the Mail icon shown here:

   The first-time Mail user's dialog box is displayed on the screen, as you see here:

3. Choose the default option, Connect to an existing postoffice, by clicking on the OK button or pressing [Enter]. The Network Disk Resources dialog box appears on your screen, as shown in Figure 7-4.

Connecting to the Postoffice

Connecting to an existing Workgroup Postoffice requires some homework to ensure that the process goes smoothly. First, you need to verify that you have the hard disk space to store your message files. Depending on the quantity of messages you hold in your mailbox, you will need anywhere from a few hundred kilobytes to several megabytes of disk space.

Using Windows for Workgroups' Mail

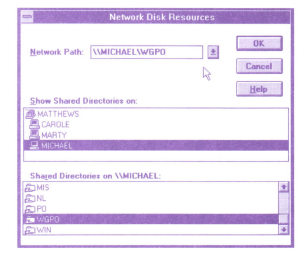

Network Disk
Resources
dialog box
Figure 7-4.

Secondly, you need to know the path to the Postoffice you are connecting to. The path consists of two pieces of information: the network computer name where the Postoffice is located (*computer name*) and the name of the shared directory or file that you want to access (*directory name*). The pathname looks like this:

*computer name**directory name*

The double backslash preceding the computer name and the single backslash separating the computer name from the shared directory name are required.

Finally, you should check with your Postoffice administrator to see if he or she has already created an account for you.

Now use one of two methods to set up your path in the Network Disk Resources dialog box:

1. In the Network Path text box, type the computer name and shared directory name with the syntax shown previously. Or, choose the computer name from the Show Shared Directories on list box, and then choose the shared directory name for your Postoffice from the Shared Directories list box. Mail will input the proper syntax for you.

2. Click on OK or press Enter. Another dialog box appears and asks if you have an account in the Postoffice you connected to.

3. Choose No to create a new account if your Postoffice administrator has not created an account for you, or choose Yes and type in your password if the Postoffice administrator has created an account for you. The Enter Your Account Details dialog box will then appear, as shown here:

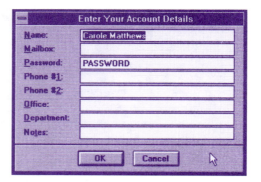

Opening a Personal Mailbox

Now that you are connected to your Workgroup Postoffice, Mail requires that you enter three items of information in the Account Details dialog box. Five other items of personal data are optional. The required information will ensure correct mail routing and confidentiality. The optional entries provide other Postoffice users information about you that may make it easier to know where you are located in the organization. This is especially useful in companies with large numbers of employees.

In the following exercise, type in the information and use the mouse pointer or Tab to move from one category to another. The Postoffice Manager is not case-sensitive so you can use either upper- or lowercase. Type information that is easy for others to read and easy for you to input.

1. Type your full name. The default is the name you used to install Windows for Workgroups. The maximum length allowed is 30 characters.

Using Windows for Workgroups' Mail

2. Type a mailbox name you will use to sign in Mail, such as your first name. The default is the name you use to log on to Windows for Workgroups. The name must be unique among members of your Postoffice. The maximum length of a mailbox name is 10 characters.

3. Type a password you will use, in conjunction with your mailbox name, to log on to Mail. The default is PASSWORD. If you don't want to use a password, press [Del] and leave the password field blank. Your password can later be changed using the Change Password option in the Mail menu. The maximum password length is 8 characters.

4. The next four entries are optional. They are your primary and alternate (or fax) phone numbers, and your office and department. The maximum length of each of these entries is 32 characters.

5. The final entry allows you to add any notes to your account. The maximum length of this field is 128 characters.

6. Press [Enter]. You are now signed in to Mail. Your Inbox opens in a small window, as shown in Figure 7-5.

Signing In

The next time you open Mail, you sign in by entering your password in the Mail Sign In dialog box, shown here:

You can have Mail automatically enter your password for you with the following steps. (If you do not want your password entered automatically, skip to the next section, "Using Your Address Book.")

1. Open Mail's Control menu box, located in the upper-left corner of the screen.

2. Choose Switch To and double-click on the Program Manager.

Networking Windows for Workgroups

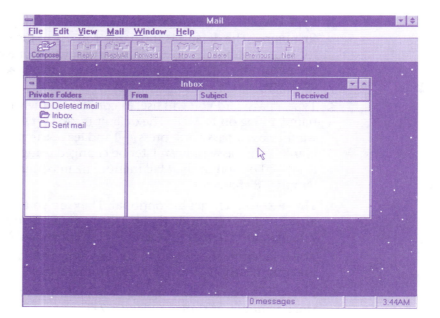

Mail's Inbox opened in a small window
Figure 7-5.

3. Choose the Mail icon in the Program Manager's Main group.
4. Choose the Properties option from the File menu.
5. In the Command Line text box, after MSMAIL.EXE, add your Mail sign-in name and password, preceding and following your name with a space. For example, MSMAIL.EXE **john dog**, where *john* is a Mail sign-in name and *dog* is a password.
6. Click on OK or press (Enter). Use the Control menu box to return to Mail.

Using the Address Book

Before you can send messages to the people in your workgroup, you need to know their mailbox names. You can type the name of the person to whom you are sending mail directly on the screen, but if you spell the name incorrectly or if the mailbox name is different from the conversational name, you won't get your message to the person. To assist you, Mail provides an Address Book that is really two directories in one. The first is the Postoffice List, which is a comprehensive list of

Using Windows for Workgroups' Mail

all the people in your Workgroup Postoffice. Depending on the size of your Postoffice, this could become quite an unwieldy list. To help you access the people you communicate with most often, Mail allows you to create a custom list, the Personal Address Book. Look at both of these directories next.

Postoffice List

To look at the Postoffice List, Mail should be on your screen and your Inbox should be open. Then use the following instructions to open the Address Book and use the Postoffice List.

1. Select Mail from the menu bar and choose Address Book. The Address Book window appears, with the Postoffice List directory opened, as shown in Figure 7-6.

   When you compose a message, you can access this list directly to select your addresses. If you have a large list of people and cannot see all of the people you need, Mail provides a search capability.

2. Click on the Search button, third from the top, in the four icons on the left side of the window. The Name Finder dialog box appears, as shown here:

   Type in as much as you know of a user's name; the more you type, the more specific the search becomes.

3. Click on Find. The name you typed, or a list of names that contain the letters you typed, appears.

4. Select the name of the user you were looking for if it isn't highlighted. Click on the Details buttons at the bottom of the Address Book window to see information about that user, such as phone number, office, and department.

5. Click on Close to return to the Find list.

6. Click on the Directory button (the top button on the left), highlight Postoffice List in the Open Directory dialog box, and click on OK.

Networking Windows for Workgroups

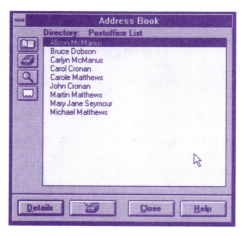

Address Book window, with the Postoffice List directory opened
Figure 7-6.

Personal Address Book

To avoid searching through a large list every time you send mail to people on a recurring basis, the Personal Address Book comes in handy.

1. Select a user from the Postoffice List to whom you send mail. Click on the Add Name button (the second button from the left at the bottom of the Address Book) to have the highlighted name added to the Personal Address Book.

2. Click on the Personal Address button (the second button from the top on the left side of the Address Book). The directory changes to the Personal Address Book and lists your own name and the name of the added user.

   As with the Postoffice List directory, you can search for people and see details on any person in the list. You can also remove any user by choosing the Remove button, which appears when you highlight someone already in your Personal Address Book.

3. Click on the Directory button (the top one on the left side). The Open Directory dialog box appears. This dialog box allows you to specify which directory will be the default when you open the Address Book. If you want the Personal Address Book to be the default, select it and click on the Set Default button. Click on OK to return to the Address Book window. Your default directory appears.

Using Windows for Workgroups' Mail

4. Click on Close. Now you are ready to address and send your first message.

Entering and Sending Your Message

Once you have identified the person to whom you want to send your message, the next step is to create the message. Follow these steps:

1. Click on the Compose button, located on the left end of Mail's button bar. The Send Note dialog box opens, as shown in Figure 7-7.
2. Click on the Address button on the right side of the Send Note dialog box. The Address Book dialog box opens with the default directory you set up in the previous section.
3. Click on the name of the person to whom you will send the note and then click on the Add: To button that you will see in the middle of the screen. The name then appears in the To text box, as shown here:

4. If you want to send a copy of your message to additional people, select those people and click on the Cc button (similar to using the To button for the addressees).

    Alternatively, you can set up a group address to send messages to a pre-established list of people. Use the Personal Groups option in

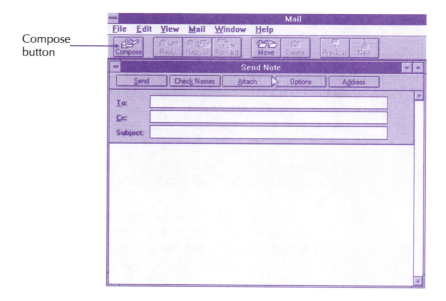

Send Note dialog box
Figure 7-7.

the Mail menu to select the people from either your Personal Address Book or Postoffice List.

5. Click on OK or press Enter to return to the Send Note dialog box.

6. Press Tab twice or click on the Subject text box to move the I-beam there. Type **First Time Message** in the box.

7. Press Tab once or click anywhere in the message area in the lower half of the window. Type **This is my first message to check some of the features used in Windows for Workgroups Mail. Talk to you later.**

8. Click on Send to finish the process.

The message text editor provides many essential editing tools, including wordwrapping, use of the File menu for copying and pasting with the Windows Clipboard, and basic text manipulation.

Three indicators inform you whether your mail has been read or not. First, the icon to the left of the message header in the Inbox shows a closed envelope if the message has not been read. Once read, the envelope appears opened. Second, the To name is in bold type if the message has not been read. Finally, if you have the status bar visible (it

Using Windows for Workgroups' Mail

is turned on or off through the View menu), it will indicate how many messages are in your Inbox and how many of them have not been read.

You can also send mail from the Windows File Manager. Selecting Mail from the menu bar and choosing Send Mail displays Mail's sign-in window (if you're not already signed in to Mail). A blank Send Note window appears if you are signed in.

Receiving Mail

When you receive mail you can read it, reply to the sender, forward it to other people, or attach files to it. Reading mail, replying to mail, and forwarding mail are discussed in this section. The last option, attaching files, is discussed in the section, "Object Embedding with Mail."

Reading Your Mail

Have another member of your workgroup send you a Mail message. You will hear a beep, and a message notification will appear in your Inbox, similar to Figure 7-8.

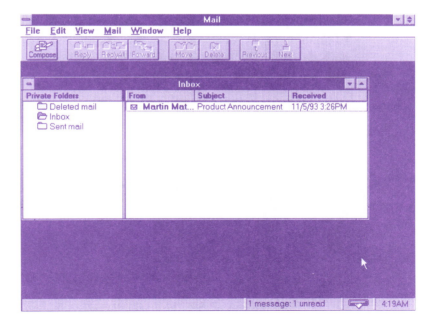

An unread message notification appears in the Inbox
Figure 7-8.

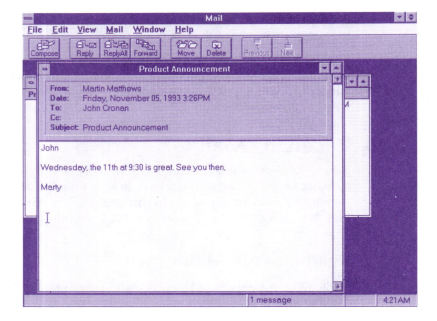

Opened
message
window
Figure 7-9.

Double-click on the message, or use [Tab] to highlight it and press [Enter] to open it. Your practice message opens in its own window, similar to Figure 7-9. Take a moment to look over the information available in the message header and then send a reply in the next section.

Replying to Mail

After reading a message, you might send a reply. You can send a reply with the message opened or with the message header highlighted in your Inbox. A reply includes the original message—a convenient feature that allows you to include your comments before, after, or within the message. The message you just received should still be on your screen.

1. Choose either the Reply button from Mail's button bar, or the Reply option from the Mail menu. A new message form appears in which Mail has added "RE:" (abbreviation for with regard to) to the

Using Windows for Workgroups' Mail

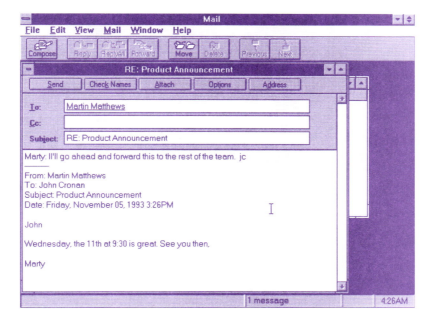

Example of a reply
Figure 7-10.

name of the original message, in both the title bar and the Subject text box. Also, the name of the sender appears in the To box.

2. Type a suitable reply. Notice the short line that separates your reply from the original message, as you can see in Figure 7-10.

3. Click on Send.

When a message has been sent not only to you, but to several recipients, you can send your reply to everyone by using the ReplyAll button in Mail's button bar or the Reply to All menu command.

Forwarding Mail

In many cases you may want to forward a copy of an existing message to one or more people. Much like replying to a message, you can add comments to the original message and attach files to an open message or one selected in your Inbox.

With the reply message still on your screen, perform the following steps to forward the message to other people in your Postoffice:

1. Click on the Forward button in Mail's button bar, or choose Forward from the Mail menu. A Send Note form appears in which Mail has added "FW:" (for forward) to the name of the original message, in both the title bar and Subject text box.

   An alternate way to forward a message is to drag the highlighted message from the Inbox to the Outbox. The Outbox temporarily holds messages and files until they can be sent by Mail. When a message is dragged to the Outbox, a Send Note form set up for forwarding is displayed.

2. Click on Address to open the Address Book. Choose a person to forward the message to, then click on the To button. Repeat this for a couple more people. Click on OK to return to the message form with the new names in the To text box.

3. Type a short message. Your note should now look similar to Figure 7-11.

4. Click on Send. The message is first sent to the Outbox and then to all the people named in the To or the Cc text box.

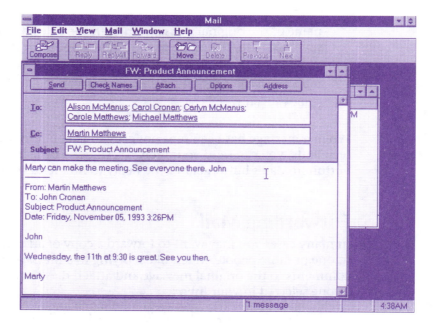

Example of a forwarded message
Figure 7-11.

Using Windows for Workgroups' Mail

Your original message remains in your Inbox where you can perform some housekeeping tasks to keep your mail organized.

Housekeeping

Mail offers a number of techniques to help you organize and manipulate your electronic correspondence, including storing your messages in folders, creating address groups, finding mail, and deleting unwanted mail.

As you can see from the few messages you've created so far, your Inbox can quickly become cluttered with messages. You have three choices: keep them in your Inbox (soon gets out of hand), file them, or delete them.

Filing Mail

Messages that you want to keep can be organized into folders. Create a folder to store your miscellaneous messages in the following exercise:

1. From the File menu, choose the New Folder option. The New Folder dialog box appears, as shown here:

2. Type **Miscellaneous** in the Name box. Choose the Type default, Private, and then click on OK. A new folder appears in the private folders area of your Inbox.

3. Drag the reply message (the one with RE: preceding the subject) from your Inbox to the new folder by grabbing the opened envelope icon and dropping it in the box that forms around the Miscellaneous folder. Notice the message is removed from the Inbox.

Alternatively, with the reply message selected, you can use the Move button in the button bar to transfer the message from one folder to another. To do this, click on the Move button, select the new folder in the Move Message dialog box, and click on OK.

4. Double-click on the Miscellaneous folder to open it. Your reply message is now stored in the folder, in the same format as in your Inbox. The only differences between open folders are their contents and titles.

The New Folder dialog box offers a choice between private and shared folders. Private means just that, only you have access. Shared folders are like shared directories, other people can access the messages they contain. You can control the degree of access by choosing the Options button in the New Folder dialog box. The expanded New Folder dialog box, shown in Figure 7-12, provides an Other Users Can area that allows you to grant read, write, or delete privileges to other people.

The expanded New Folder dialog box and the File menu's Folder Properties dialog box also let you assign folders as top-level folders or subfolders, which is analogous to creating directories and subdirectories.

Expanded New Folder dialog box with Other Users Can area
Figure 7-12.

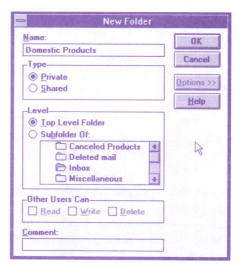

Using Windows for Workgroups' Mail

Creating Address Groups

There are many occasions when you will send messages and attached files to a group of Postoffice users on a recurring basis. Instead of using your Personal Address Book and repeatedly finding and choosing the same group of people each time you send a message, you can create an *address group* that contains the user's names, and mail your message to them all at once.

You can create several address groups that cover, for instance, your department, each division in your department, and others based on projects or process action teams that cross organization lines. Some people may appear in only one address group; others may appear in every address group.

The Personal Groups dialog boxes easily guide you through the steps to create an address group. Use the following exercise to create one now:

1. Choose Personal Groups from the Mail menu. Click on New in the Personal Groups dialog box.
2. In the New Group dialog box, provide a name for the group. Click on Create. A dialog box similar to the Address Book dialog box appears, as shown in Figure 7-13.

Personal Groups dialog box
Figure 7-13.

3. Select a person from the Postoffice List, click on Add, and repeat the process for each member of the address group. As you add new people, their names appear in the Group Members text box. When you are finished, click on OK. You are returned to the Personal Groups dialog box with your new address group selected.

4. Click on Close.

Finding Mail

After you've created a number of folders and filed your messages in an orderly fashion, how do you find the minutes of your last meeting that the boss wants now, when they're not in the Minutes folder? It's simple—invoke Message Finder, Mail's convenient message search feature.

Open the Miscellaneous folder containing the reply message you placed there earlier, and follow these steps:

1. Choose Message Finder in the File menu. The Message Finder dialog box appears, as shown here:

2. Press [Tab] three times or click on the Message Text box and type some text that is in the body of the message. (You could just as easily search on text you type in the From, Subject, or Recipients text box to find your message.)

3. Click on the Where to Look button and choose Look in all folders from the dialog box. Then click on OK.

4. Click on Start in the Message Finder dialog box that reappears. The message that contains the search words appears in the lower half

Using Windows for Workgroups' Mail

of the dialog box. The Message Finder includes the normal header information for each message and the folder where each is located. Double-click on the message header of the message to see it.

5. Double-click on the Control menu box to close Message Finder and return to the Miscellaneous folder. The reply message should still be highlighted.

Deleting Mail

The final housekeeping feature deals with deleting unwanted mail. You can delete mail from your Inbox or any of the folders you create. Deleted mail is not permanently removed; it is moved to the Deleted Mail folder. Deleted mail stays in the Deleted Mail folder until you exit Mail; then it is permanently deleted. You can change the default setting so deleted mail isn't removed when you exit Mail by opening the Mail menu, choosing Options, and clicking on the Other check box.

1. Click on the Delete button in the button bar. The reply message is removed from the Miscellaneous folder.

2. Double-click on the Deleted Mail folder in the Folders area of the window. The Deleted Mail folder opens with the reply message listed in the header area, as shown here:

You can move mail from the Deleted Mail folder to another folder by dragging the message's envelope icon or by using the Move button in the button bar.

Printing Messages

You can obtain hard copies of your messages simply by sending them to a printer. To do this, select the messages to be printed by clicking on them (hold down Ctrl to select several messages), then choose Print from the File menu. Ensure that your setup is correct, and send the message or messages to your printer. Messages can be printed when opened or when selected in a folder.

Quitting Mail

There are two options on the File menu to exit Mail. The first option, Exit, closes Mail to a standby status, but still allows you to use other applications that use Mail to communicate with members of your workgroup. Schedule+, discussed in Chapter 8, is one such application. The second option, Exit and Sign Out, exits you from Mail and closes Mail completely. In order to access another application that uses Mail, you have to sign into Mail again.

At this point, you can exit Mail. The next three sections discuss more advanced uses of Mail. The exercises do not have to be completed in any order; you can do them as you need them.

Creating Mail Templates

If you send a recurring message with contents that remain nearly the same, consider saving the basic form as a *template* to eliminate retyping a majority of the contents each time. Some examples of messages you can use templates for are attendance reports, budget reviews, and production reports. To create a template, follow these steps:

1. Create the initial message using the Compose button or the Mail menu command. Address it to your anticipated audience and complete the permanent body of the template.

2. Double-click on the Control menu box. Choose Yes when asked if you want to save the message. The message is saved to your Inbox. You may find it convenient to create a Template folder and store all your forms there.

3. Forward the message either by choosing the Forward menu command or by dragging the message to the Outbox.

Using Windows for Workgroups' Mail

4. Fill in the pertinent information. You can modify your addressees as the need arises.
5. Click on the Send button.

Working with Mail Offline

You can create messages or modify existing messages even when you are not connected to your Workgroup Postoffice. You need two items: a computer that has Windows for Workgroups and Mail installed, and a disk copy of your MSMAIL.MMF file. The MSMAIL.MMF file contains your messages, folders, and Personal Address Book.

If you start Mail when you are not connected to your Postoffice, a dialog box is displayed asking if you would like to work offline. Choosing Yes displays the Sign In window and prompts for your password. After you sign in, if Mail cannot find your MSMAIL.MMF file, it will ask you for its path.

Send mail you create or modify as you normally would, by choosing the Send button. The messages are moved to your Outbox. When you connect to the Postoffice, Mail will send any messages in your Outbox to the recipients.

Attaching Files to Mail

Along with your messages, you can send data and program files by attaching them to a message. Files can be attached to send, reply, and forwarded messages. To attach files to new or existing messages, use the following steps:

1. Within the message text area, move the insertion point to where you want the attached file icon to appear. If you don't specify a location, the icon is placed at the beginning of the message.

NOTE: The program uses the standard Windows icons to identify the files, such as those for Word documents and PageMaker documents.

2. Click on the Attach button. The Attach dialog box opens, as shown here:

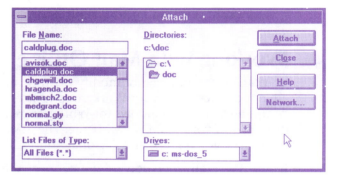

Either type the path of the attached file in the File Name text box or use the Directories, Drives, and File Name list boxes to find your file. Double-click on the filename in the list box or click on the Attach button to have the file's icon and filename included in the message. You can attach as many files as your system memory allows. Click on Close when you are finished. Figure 7-14 shows a message with multiple attached files as icons.

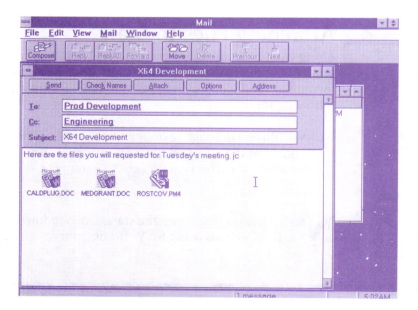

Attached file icons in a message
Figure 7-14.

If you receive a message and want to view an attached unformatted text (ASCII) file, double-click on the file icon. Or press (Shift) and any arrow key to select the icon, and then use the File Open dialog box to open the file. ASCII files are opened in the Windows Notebook.

Non-ASCII files first need to be saved and then opened from their respective application programs. Save attached files with the following steps:

1. Choose the Save Attachment option from the File menu. The Save Attachment dialog box opens, as shown here:

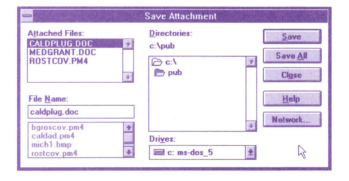

2. The attached file is saved to the current directory by choosing the Save button. Multiple attachments can be saved simultaneously by clicking on the Save All button. If you want to save the file under a different filename, or in a different directory, use the list boxes and File Name text box to create the path.
3. Click on the Close button when you are finished saving the attachments.

Object Embedding with Mail

Your Mail messages can have embedded objects (graphics or formatted text) that are created in application programs. Unlike a Clipboard copy and paste, embedding establishes a connection between Mail and the application program that created the object. This connection allows you to modify the object in Mail by simply double-clicking on it. An embedded object is a copy of the original; modifications to the embedded object do not change the original. Mail does not allow linking objects, only embedding.

The following steps illustrate the embedding process:

1. From a Send Note form, move the insertion point to the location in the message text area where you want the object.

2. Choose Insert Object from the Edit menu. The Insert Object dialog box appears with a list of your programs that are OLE (object linking and embedding) compatible. Select the program you want to use.

3. The application program opens so you can create the object.

4. Choose Update from the File menu or close the application. The object is inserted into your message.

5. To modify the object, double-click on it. Its application program opens with the object in a window, ready for editing.

6. After you make your modifications, choose the File Update command or close the program. The changes you make appear in your Mail message.

If you have an existing object you want to embed in a message use these steps:

1. Copy the object to the Clipboard from its application program.

2. Switch to Mail using the Switch To option in the application's Control menu box. Or, press and hold ⟦Alt⟧ while pressing ⟦Tab⟧ to rotate through the open programs.

3. Click on the Compose button.

4. Choose Paste Special from the Edit menu. Select the object format from the Data Type dialog box.

5. Choose the Paste button to embed the object.

The Workgroup Postoffice Administrator

The remainder of this chapter explains the role of the Workgroup Postoffice administrator. This person creates the Postoffice, adds and

Using Windows for Workgroups' Mail

removes users, and otherwise ensures the smooth operation of the Postoffice.

Setting Up the Workgroup Postoffice

The Windows for Workgroups Mail facility is composed of two distinct features: the Workgroup Postoffice and the Mail application itself. The Workgroup Postoffice is only available to the Postoffice administrator; the Mail application is loaded on each computer in the workgroup.

The administrator's first responsibility is to verify that there is adequate disk space to support Mail. The recommended available disk space for the administrator is 360K for the empty Postoffice and 16K for each user. Individual users need approximately 100K of disk space for a small mailbox; several megabytes should be allotted for larger mailboxes.

Another responsibility of the administrator is to ensure that his or her computer is turned on whenever there is an opportunity for people to transfer mail. If it is not on, users are limited to composing messages and modifying received mail; they cannot send or receive mail.

Setting Up the Postoffice Administration Account

The first person to join the Postoffice must be its administrator. Create a Postoffice Administration Account with the following instructions:

1. Start Mail from the Program Manager's Main group. The Welcome to Mail dialog box appears, as shown here:

2. Choose the Create a new Workgroup Postoffice option. Click on OK and then Yes in the dialog box that follows.

3. The Create Workgroup Postoffice dialog box opens, allowing you to change the default drive and directory of the Postoffice. Accept the default settings by clicking on OK.

4. The Administrator Account dialog box opens. Enter the personal information that Mail uses to identify you to the system and other users.

4. Type your full name. The default is the name you used to install Windows for Workgroups. The maximum length of the name is 30 characters.

5. Type a mailbox name you will use to sign in to Mail, such as your first name. The default is the name you use to log on to Windows for Workgroups. The name must be unique among members of your Postoffice. The maximum length of this name is 10 characters.

6. Type a password you will use, in conjunction with your mailbox name, to log on to Mail. The default is PASSWORD. Press Del if you do not want a password. A password can later be changed by choosing the Change Password option in the Mail menu. The maximum length of the password is 8 characters.

7. The next four optional entries are your primary and alternate (or fax) phone numbers, and your office and department. The maximum length of these fields is 32 characters each.

8. The final entry allows you to add any notes to your account. The notes can be up to 128 characters long. Type them now and then press Enter.

Sharing the Workgroup Postoffice

Now that you've created the Postoffice, you must share it with the workgroup users.

1. Click on OK to indicate that you will share the Workgroup Postoffice directory with other users.

2. Switch to the File Manager and highlight your \WGPO\ directory. If you set up the Postoffice in a different directory, highlight that directory.

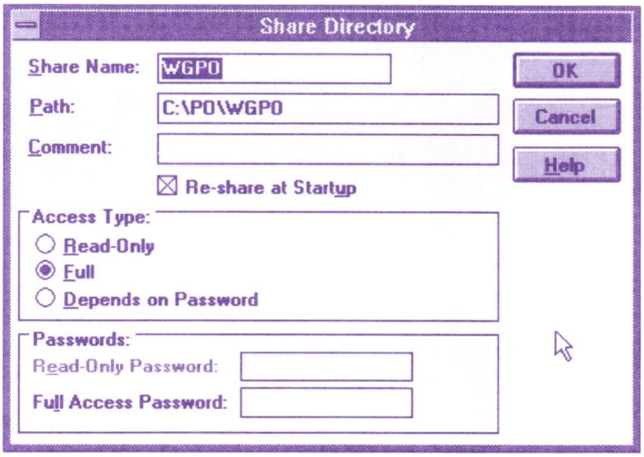

Using Windows for Workgroups' Mail

195

Share Directory
dialog box
Figure 7-15.

3. Choose Share As from the Disk menu. The Share Directory dialog box opens, as shown in Figure 7-15.

4. Accept the default Share Name and Path, and ensure that the Re-share at Startup check box is selected.

5. Choose the Full option button in the Access Type box.

6. Click on OK and switch back to Mail.

Setting Up Individual Accounts

The administrator is the only person who has the Postoffice Manager option available in the Mail menu. Postoffice Manager allows the administrator to see a list of all users in the workgroup and add, remove, and change user accounts.

Open the Postoffice Manager by clicking on the Postoffice Manager option in the Mail menu. The dialog box shown in Figure 7-16 appears.

Adding an Account

Adding a user is similar to setting up the administrator account. The same information is requested. Individual users can set up their own accounts, but it may make more sense, depending on the size and computer knowledge of the workgroup, for the administrator to perform account setups and changes. To add a user:

Networking Windows for Workgroups

1. Click on the Add User button. The Add User dialog box appears, as shown here:

2. Fill in the appropriate information, using the instructions in the section, "Setting Up the Postoffice Administration Account," as a guide.
3. Choose OK to enter the settings.

Modifying an Account

The administrator can change user information on any existing account. To modify a user's account, follow these steps:

1. From the list of users in the Postoffice Manager dialog box, select the user account you want to modify.

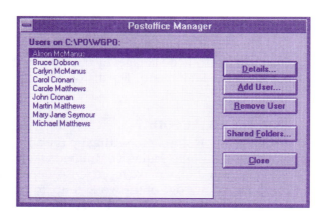

Postoffice Manager dialog box
Figure 7-16.

Using Windows for Workgroups' Mail

2. Click on the Details button. The user's personal information appears in a dialog box.

3. Make the necessary changes, and choose OK when you're finished.

Removing an Account

1. From the list of users in the Postoffice Manager dialog box, select the user account you want to remove. You cannot remove the administrator's account.

2. Click on the Remove User button. A dialog box opens with the user's name and asks if you're sure you want to remove it.

3. Click on Yes.

Maintaining the Postoffice Files

Any user can create shared folders that all users in the workgroup can access. These shared folders are stored in the Postoffice on the administrator's computer. Private folders are stored on each user's computer. Depending on the number of shared folders, the number of files in the folders, the size of the files, and the amount of available disk space, the data in the files may need to be compressed. Additionally, as the administrator, you may be called upon to back up Postoffice files or change the name, location, and existence of the workgroup.

Determining the Status of Postoffice Files

The first step in performing disk space management is determining the status of Postoffice files. The Postoffice Manager provides much useful information, including:

✦ The number of shared folders

✦ The number of messages contained in the shared folders

✦ The total amount of disk space occupied by all messages

✦ The amount of disk space compressing the files would save

If you decide to compress shared folders after analyzing their status, be aware of a few considerations: First, do not compress folders while people are using them. In a large workgroup you may need to schedule maintenance periods to perform this task. Second, remember that compressing larger messages can take considerable time. Finally, after compressing the folders, you may not recover all the disk space you need. You might have to delete some messages and folders, add additional disk space, or move the Postoffice to a computer that has more disk space.

Compressing Postoffice Files

The easiest solution to the need for more disk space is to compress the existing files so that they take less room on the disk. Use the following instructions to try out the file compression. (You'll need some messages in your shared folders to try this.)

1. Click on the Shared Folders button. The Shared Folders dialog box opens, as shown below:

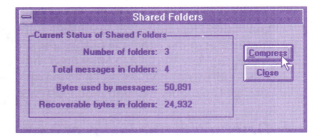

2. Choose the Compress button. When the compression process is complete, click on Close.

Backing Up and Restoring Postoffice Files

Two files are vital to the continued success of your Postoffice—MSMAIL.INI and MSMAIL.MMF. Backing up these two files allows you to recover the Mail setup and messages up to a given point, in case of problems with the original files. The administrator should ensure that the members of the workgroup are familiar with backup procedures and that they back up their files on a recurring schedule.

Using Windows for Workgroups' Mail

MSMAIL.INI   Back up your MSMAIL.INI file simply by using the File Manager to copy the file to a new file with a different name; then copy this file to a floppy disk. Some examples of alternate names are: MSMAIL.001, MSMAIL.OLD, and MSMAIL.BAK. If something happens to your original MSMAIL.INI file, you can restore it by renaming the backup file MSMAIL.INI and moving it to its original location.

MSMAIL.MMF   The MSMAIL.MMF file contains all the messages in your private folders. When you back up this file, all messages and folders are backed up. Individual folders can be backed up or restored by using the Export and Import commands in the File menu. To back up your MSMAIL.MMF file:

1. Choose Backup from the Mail menu. The Backup dialog box opens.
2. Either use the Directories and Drives boxes or type the path and name of your backup file in the File Name box.
3. Choose OK to perform the backup.

To restore your MSMAIL.MMF file if something goes wrong with the original:

1. Using the File Manager, choose Rename from the File menu.
2. Type c:\windows\msmail.mmf in the To box and click on OK. The folders and messages that were in your backup file now become your current mailbox.

Modifying the Workgroup Postoffice

There are several modifications that you can make to your Workgroup Postoffice as a whole. These include changing the Postoffice name, moving the Postoffice, and deleting a Postoffice. Look at each of these tasks in the next several sections. Whenever you make major changes to the Postoffice, first ensure that all users are signed off of Mail.

Changing Your Postoffice Name   You should not need to change the Postoffice name unless the original name no longer applies to the function of the workgroup, or you join, or are joined by, a workgroup of the same name. To change the Postoffice name, follow these steps:

1. Using the File Manager, select the WGPO directory.

2. Choose Share As from the Disk menu. Type the new Postoffice name in the Share Name box.

3. Choose OK to rename the Postoffice directory.

4. Use Windows Notepad to open the administrator's MSMAIL.INI file. Then, in the [Microsoft Mail] area, change the ServerPath= line to reflect the new name.

5. Advise the other users in the workgroup of the new name and ask them to use Notepad to change the ServerPath= line in their MSMAIL.INI file to reflect the new Postoffice directory.

Moving Your Postoffice   You may want to move the Postoffice because you get a new or larger computer, or for another reason. To move the Postoffice, use the following instructions:

1. Using the File Manager, select the WGPO directory.

2. Choose Move from the File menu. Type the new path in the To box and click on OK.

3. Set up the new Postoffice as a shared directory using the Share As option in the File Manager's Disk menu.

4. In the administrator's MSMAIL.INI file, [Microsoft Mail] area, change the ServerPath= line to reflect the new location.

5. Advise the other users in the workgroup of the new location and ask them to change their ServerPath= line to reflect it.

Deleting Your Postoffice   If you join another Postoffice, you may want to delete your Postoffice. To do that, use these steps:

1. Using the File Manager, delete the WGPO directories and subdirectories.

2. Rename MSMAIL.INI file MSMAIL.OLD. The next time you use Mail, MSMAIL.INI will be re-created. After you are sure your new MSMAIL.INI file is what you want to use, you can delete MSMAIL.OLD.

Other Networks and Mail

Your Workgroup Postoffice, as well as your own workgroup files, can be placed on the servers of other networks. Use of two of the most popular

Using Windows for Workgroups' Mail

networks, Novell's NetWare and Microsoft's LAN Manager, is discussed in the following sections.

Novell's NetWare

Create a Workgroup Postoffice on the NetWare server using the following steps:

1. Open the Control Panel's Network settings and click on Networks. Select Novell NetWare, click on Add, and then on OK to provide NetWare support from Windows for Workgroups.
2. Start Windows for Workgroups after logging on to the NetWare server.
3. Using the File Manager, assign a drive letter to the NetWare directory where you want to create the Postoffice.
4. Create a Postoffice as you normally would.

Microsoft's LAN Manager

LAN Manager doesn't require special support for use with Windows for Workgroups Mail. You just have to create a Postoffice on a LAN Manager server, share the Postoffice directory, and offer full access. Additionally, to view the LAN Manager servers in the Connect and Share dialog box, ensure that one workgroup computer's workgroup name matches the name of the primary domain controller on the server.

Other Networks

Similar to using Windows for Workgroups with NetWare, other networks can be set up using the Control Panel Network icon. Consult your network documentation or vendor for information concerning the network drivers needed to use Windows for Workgroups.

Troubleshooting

From time to time, problems might crop up concerning the Workgroup Postoffice or user accounts. The administrator can eliminate many problems by taking an active role in managing the Postoffice. The larger the workgroup and the more each user tries to customize or "fix" their mailbox, the greater the opportunity for something to go wrong.

One of the most common problems is for a person to forget his or her password. As long as the person is not the administrator, this is easily fixed. Just create a new password for that person from the Postoffice Manager's Detail dialog box. If you, the administrator, forget your password, you will need to create a new Postoffice.

If you cannot create a Postoffice, there can be several reasons why you're having trouble. You may not have enough disk space. See the section, "Compressing Postoffice Files," for help in extracting more disk space. Also, if you're trying to create a workgroup on a server, ensure that you have write permission on the server.

Mail Help is probably the most convenient source for solutions to day-to-day problems. Help is available from the Mail menu or many dialog boxes.

In the next chapter you'll look at how Mail's features combine with Schedule+ to make a powerful appointment book and planner. You will also learn to use three Windows for Workgroups accessories that are specifically for networking: Chat, Net Watcher, and WinMeter.

CHAPTER

8

USING WINDOWS FOR WORKGROUPS' SCHEDULE+ AND OTHER ACCESSORIES

This chapter explores the uses of networking beyond just transferring messages and files. The main focus is Schedule+, an interactive program that allows network users to set up individual appointment calendars and task listings, and then coordinate their schedule with other members of the workgroup in order to jointly schedule meetings. Following the discussion of Schedule+, three applications from the Windows for Workgroups Accessories group, Chat, Net Watcher, and WinMeter, are described. Chat is an onscreen communicator—it lets you and another person on the network type notes to each other and have them appear onscreen as they are being typed. Net Watcher allows you to monitor how the network's resources, and your own directories and files, are being used by others. The chapter concludes with WinMeter, a facility that gives you a graphic measurement of the demand on your computer, both by you and other workgroup members.

Introducing Schedule+

Schedule+ is composed of four utilities, all aimed at improving time management. From the convenience of your computer, you can maintain an appointment book, prepare a task list, plan future events, and jointly arrange meetings with others in your workgroup, avoiding phone calls and memoranda. The next sections introduce each of these four utilities as well as the Schedule+ Help facility.

Your Appointment Book

The Appointment Book is at the heart of Schedule+. This daily scheduling tool allows you to set up your appointments in a convenient and organized manner. Figure 8-1 gives an example of a day's schedule. You have great flexibility in how you create your appointments. They can be created for any time of the day and for any duration. If you have recurring events, simply establish the initial appointment, and Schedule+ will automatically schedule the following appointments for you at the interval you desire.

Appointments indicate to other workgroup users that you are busy during a certain block of time. Without having to contact you directly, they know you are unavailable. By designating an appointment as *tentative,* other users see that time period as open and available for scheduling. You can have a total of six appointments, either standard or tentative, for a given time period. Also, you can select which, if any, users have access to your Appointment Book.

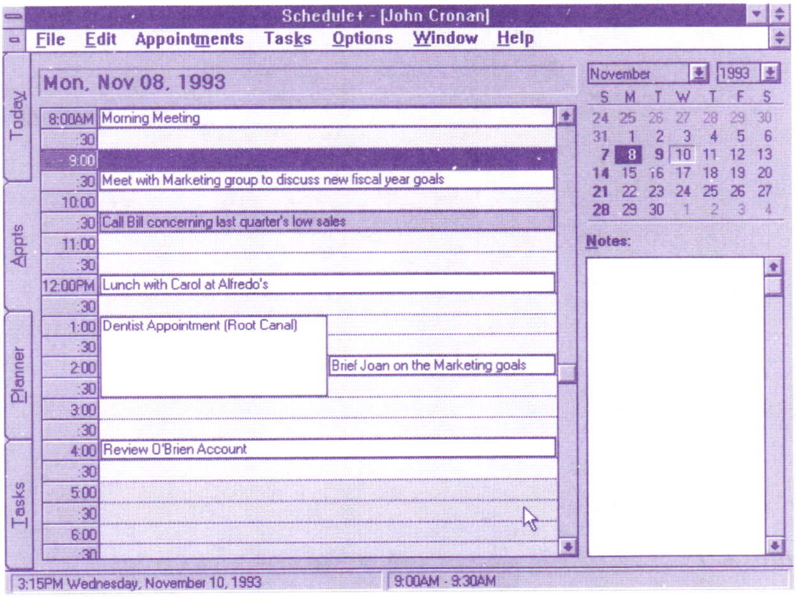

Using Windows for Workgroups' Schedule+ and Other Accessories

Schedule+ - [John Cronan]

File   Edit   Appointments   Tasks   Options   Window   Help

Mon, Nov 08, 1993

8:00AM	Morning Meeting
:30	
9:00	
:30	Meet with Marketing group to discuss new fiscal year goals
10:00	
:30	Call Bill concerning last quarter's low sales
11:00	
:30	
12:00PM	Lunch with Carol at Alfredo's
:30	
1:00	Dentist Appointment (Root Canal)
:30	
2:00	Brief Joan on the Marketing goals
:30	
3:00	
:30	
4:00	Review O'Brien Account
:30	
5:00	
:30	
6:00	
:30	

November   1993
S M T W T F S
24 25 26 27 28 29 30
31 1 2 3 4 5 6
 7 8 9 10 11 12 13
14 15 16 17 18 19 20
21 22 23 24 25 26 27
28 29 30 1 2 3 4

Notes:

3:15PM Wednesday, November 10, 1993   9:00AM - 9:30AM

Appointment
Book
Figure 8-1.

Schedule+ provides an alarm to remind you of upcoming appointments. You can select whether you are reminded of individual appointments or all appointments, and you can change how much in advance of the appointment the reminder appears. Also, the Appointment Book lets you quickly view the daily schedule of any date from 1920 to 2019 with a calendar. Simply by clicking on the day of month and opening the month and year drop-down list boxes, you can select the desired date. Finally, the calendar lets you write notes for any given day in that day's Notes box.

The Task List

The Schedule+ task list provides you with an easy-to-use tool to assist you in setting task priorities, grouping tasks into projects, establishing completion dates, and interfacing with your Appointment Book. You can sort through your projects and tasks alphabetically, by due date, or by priority. Figure 8-2 illustrates a typical task list.

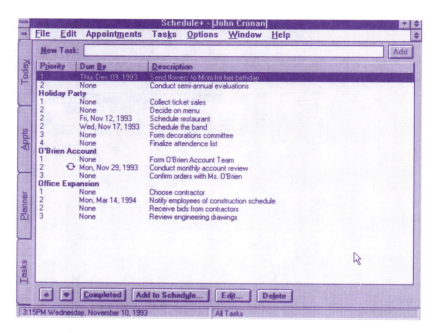

Task list
Figure 8-2.

The Planner

With the Schedule+ Planner you can see a graphic representation of your schedule and those of other workgroup members over a two-and-a-half-week period. You can easily determine when people have free time in their Appointment Books. Schedule+ assigns a different color to the time blocks of each workgroup member to allow you to compare your schedule against theirs. Overlapping time blocks are indicated by diagonal stripes. Figure 8-3 shows a Planner using the default colors, blue for the Planner owner (black on a black-and-white screen) and gray for other workgroup members.

Arranging Meetings

Working in conjunction with Windows for Workgroups' Mail, Schedule+ allows you to arrange meetings by sending and receiving messages. These messages appear in both Mail's Inbox and the Schedule+ message window. You can read, answer, or delete the messages from either application. The message notification indicates whether the person is planning on attending the meeting.

Using Windows for Workgroups' Schedule+ and Other Accessories

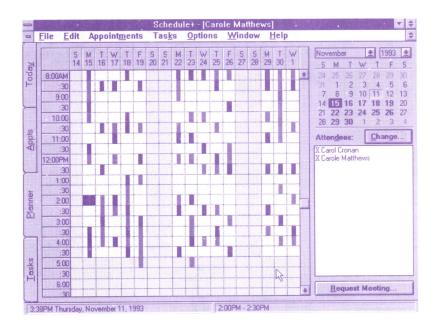

Planner
Figure 8-3.

Schedule+ automatically makes an entry in your Appointment Book and sends an affirmative reply to the sender when you accept a meeting. If you decline to attend the meeting, the sender is notified, but no change is made to your Appointment Book. Tentative acceptance lets the sender know you might attend the meeting and assigns a tentative appointment in your Appointment Book.

Schedule+ Help

Schedule+ Help uses the Windows Help facility you learned about in Chapter 2 and Mail Help discussed in Chapter 7. By pressing F1, choosing the Contents option from the Help menu, or by clicking on the Help button offered in some dialog boxes, the Schedule+ Help Contents window appears, as shown in Figure 8-4.

The major topics of Schedule+ Help are listed in the opening window. The + command button to the left of each topic displays the subtopics associated with that topic. These subtopics can also be accessed by using the Tab key to select a topic and then pressing Enter.

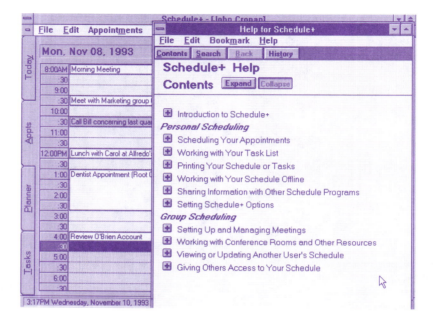

Schedule+ Help Contents window
Figure 8-4.

Alternatively, you can view the topics and all of their subtopics on the screen by choosing the Expand button under the title.

Each subtopic provides information and step-by-step procedures on how to perform a task. Also, each subtopic screen contains an Overview button that offers a brief synopsis of the topic. Underlined keywords and related topics and subtopics can be chosen to further enhance your knowledge on a specific subject. For example, Figure 8-5 shows what displays after choosing the Working with Your Task List topic, then choosing the Adding a Recurring Task subtopic, and clicking on the Overview button.

Finally, by choosing the Search button on the Schedule+ Help button bar, you can access an index of topics by scrolling through the list or by typing the topic in question. The more you type, the more specific the search becomes. Choosing the Show Topics button provides a list of suggested topics. You can then select the topic of your choice and by pressing Go To, have the topic description open.

In the next several sections, you will perform exercises using Schedule+. To prepare for that, turn on your computer, if it isn't already turned on,

Using Windows for Workgroups' Schedule+ and Other Accessories

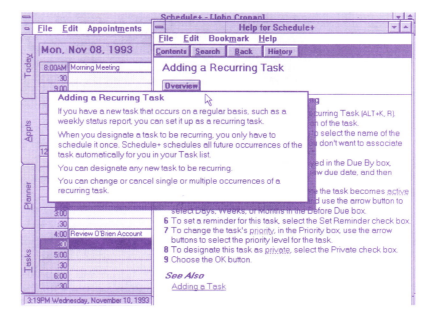

Schedule+ Help components
Figure 8-5.

start Windows if necessary, and have the Windows Program Manager on your screen.

Using Your Appointment Book

To use Schedule+, you first need to sign into Windows for Workgroups' Mail. Schedule+ uses Mail to communicate with the other users in your workgroup. Use the following steps to open Schedule+:

1. Open the Program Manager's Main group if it isn't already open.
2. Double-click on the Schedule+ icon. The Mail Sign In dialog box opens, as shown here:

3. Sign in using your Mail password, and then click on OK or press [Enter]. A message window momentarily appears on the screen. This would remain open if you had any Schedule+ messages (covered in the later section, "Using Schedule+ to Arrange Meetings"). Schedule+ now opens to the screen shown in Figure 8-6.

4. Maximize Schedule+ by clicking on the maximize button in the upper-right corner of its window.

Schedule+ is arranged like most Windows programs. The title bar contains the program name and your name as the currently opened schedule. The menu bar has four standard Windows menus—File, Edit, Window, and Help—and three menus unique to Schedule+—Appointments, Tasks, and Options. The Appointment Book and calendar are the default features that appear in the Schedule+ window. The four tabs along the left side of the Appointment Book let you easily move from one feature to another by simply clicking on a tab. Since Schedule+ opens by default to today's date in the Appointment Book, both of those tabs, Appts and Today, are on top.

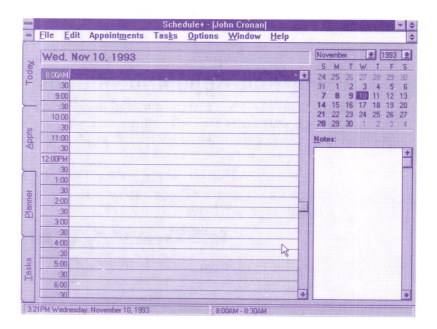

Schedule+ opening screen
Figure 8-6.

Changing Defaults

The default week starts on a Sunday and the workday is from 8:00 a.m. to 5:00 p.m. Change the starting day of the week and the time that appears at the beginning of your Appointment Book using the steps that follow:

1. Open the Options menu and choose the General Options command. The General Options dialog box opens, as shown in Figure 8-7.
2. Use your mouse pointer or [Tab] to select the hour in the Day Starts at text box. Click on the up or down arrow to obtain the correct hour. Repeat the process for the Day Starts at minutes. Notice they change in increments of 15 minutes.
3. Again, use the mouse pointer or press [Tab] to move to the Day Ends at text box. Change the ending hour and minutes as you did in step 2.
4. Press [Tab] to move to the Week Starts on drop-down list box. Click on the down arrow to display the days of the week and select which day you want the week to begin on. Before you close the dialog box, click on the check box to the left of Set Reminders Automatically, in the Reminders area, to turn it off. (Reminders will be discussed later in this section.)

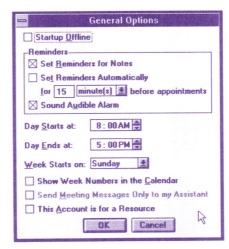

General Options dialog box
Figure 8-7.

5. Click on OK. Figure 8-8 shows an Appointment Book and calendar for someone on a swing shift starting the week on Monday.

The next section uses the default starting and ending day times, 8:00 a.m. and 5:00 p.m., and Sunday as the beginning of the week. If you changed your schedule, you might want to return to the default settings to more easily follow along.

Adding Appointments

There are three ways to add an appointment. The first two allow you to use a full-featured dialog box. The third way lets you type your appointment directly in its time slot without benefit of customization.

Use the following steps to see how easy it is to use Schedule+ to organize your appointments and events.

1. Using the current date, open the Appointments menu and choose the first option, New Appointment. The Appointment dialog box appears, as shown in Figure 8-9.

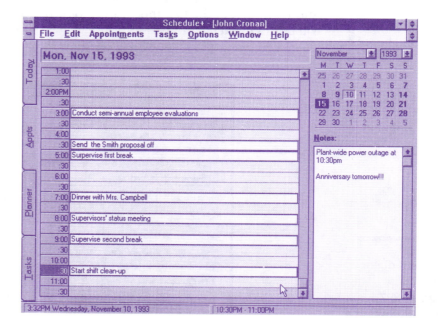

Appointment Book set up for someone on a swing shift starting the week on a Monday
Figure 8-8.

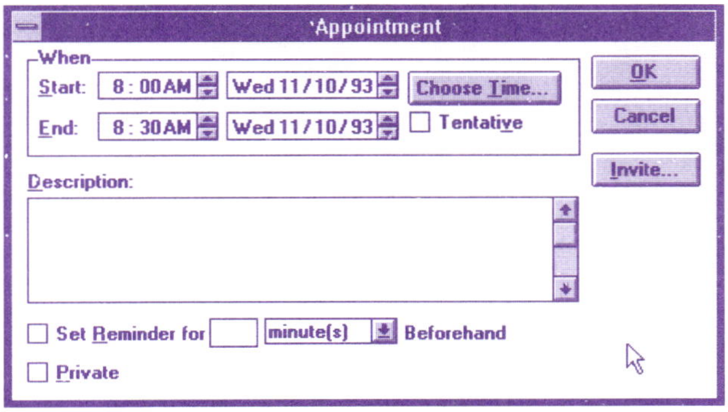

Using Windows for Workgroups' Schedule+ and Other Accessories   **215**

Appointment
dialog box
Figure 8-9.

In the When area of the dialog box, you should see the default time, 8:00 a.m., and the current date in the Start time and date boxes. The End time is 8:30 a.m., which reflects the 30-minute default time Schedule+ allots for each appointment. The End date is the current date.

2. Using the mouse pointer, either drag across the Start hour to select it and type **4**, or use the up arrow to change the 8 to a 4. Notice that a.m. changes to p.m. when you get to 12. Do the same with End, changing it to 4:30 p.m.

3. Click on the Start date day of the week (Wednesday in Figure 8-9). Use the up and down arrows to change the day. Notice as you change the day, the date also changes. In the date string, select the day (the 10th in Figure 8-9). Again, use the arrows to change the day and to see how, as the date changes, so does the rest of the date string (if you cross into another month or year) and the day of the week. Return to the current date when you are finished.

4. Click in the Description text box. This is the area where you label your appointments and events. Type **Review O'Brien Account**. There is room to write a lengthy description, but your Appointment Book will begin to look very cluttered if you don't exercise some brevity. Your dialog box should now look like the one shown in Figure 8-10.

5. Click on OK. Your Appointment Book should now look like Figure 8-11.

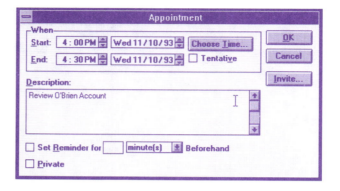

Appointment dialog box with the When and Description text boxes filled in
Figure 8-10.

The status bar at the bottom of the screen displays the current time and date, as well as the time and duration of the entry. Note the borders on the top and bottom of the 4:00 p.m. entry. See how they are used in the following steps:

1. Point on the upper border (looks similar to a thin title bar) of the 4:00 p.m. entry. The mouse pointer changes to a small

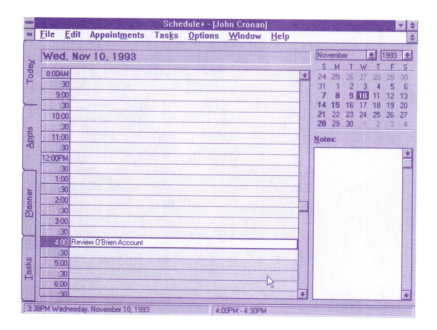

Appointment Book with a 4:00 p.m. entry
Figure 8-11.

Using Windows for Workgroups' Schedule+ and Other Accessories

double-headed arrow, as shown here:

2. Drag the border back to the 8:00 a.m. time slot. This is the fastest way to move an entry within its current day. You can also move and copy entries by selecting an entry and using the Move, Copy, and Paste menu commands. This is the preferred way to move or copy to another date.

3. Drag the lower border down to expand the description box. If you want to create a long description, you can easily see the entire entry's text.

The second way to open the Appointment dialog box and add an appointment is to go to the time slot you want and double-click in its box. First, return the Review O'Brien Account entry to its normal size. If the two borders are not visible, click on the entry to display them. Now follow these steps:

1. Above the calendar, click on the arrow to open the drop-down list box showing the current month. Change the month to October (change it to November if October is your current month) by clicking on the month's name.

2. Click on a different day in the calendar. Schedule+ quickly changes the Appointment Book to whatever day you choose. For this exercise, finish by clicking on 25. The daily schedule for the 25th of October in your current year should be on your screen, as shown here:

An alternate way to get to a given date is to use the Go To Date option in the Edit menu. The Go To Date dialog box opens, and you can either type the date or use the up or down arrow to increase or decrease the date until you get the date you want. Then by clicking on OK, Schedule+ will display the schedule for that date.

3. Double-click in the 10:00 a.m. time slot. The Appointment dialog box opens, identical to the one displayed from the Appointments menu. Type **Finalize the O'Brien Account** in the Description text box. Click on OK.

4. Notice now that you are not at the current date and the Today tab is no longer on top. Return to the current date by clicking on the Today tab.

The final way to make entries in the Appointment Book is to select the time slot you want and type in the appropriate appointment. This is by far the fastest way to make entries, as long as you can accept the default settings for some features. (These features will be discussed in the following sections.) Use this direct method in the following steps:

1. Return the Review O'Brien Account to its original 4:00 p.m. time slot.

2. Click on the 8:00 a.m. time slot and type **Morning Meeting** Then, using Figure 8-12 as a guide, complete the rest of the day's schedule by clicking on the time slot, or double-click to open the Appointments dialog box and type in the Description text box.

   Looking at the schedule, a few things should probably be changed: whoever heard of a 30-minute root canal appointment, and do you really want other users to know you have to remind yourself to brush your teeth?

3. Double-click on the 1:00 p.m. dental appointment. Change the End time to 3:00 p.m. and close the dialog box. Notice how the 2:00 p.m. appointment is moved to the side and the extended dental appointment now covers a two-hour period.

4. Highlight the comment concerning brushing your teeth by dragging across it. Choose Cut from the Edit menu, click on the Notes box, and then choose Paste from the Edit menu.

The personal comment is removed from your Appointment Book, where others could see it, and it is transferred to a daily note,

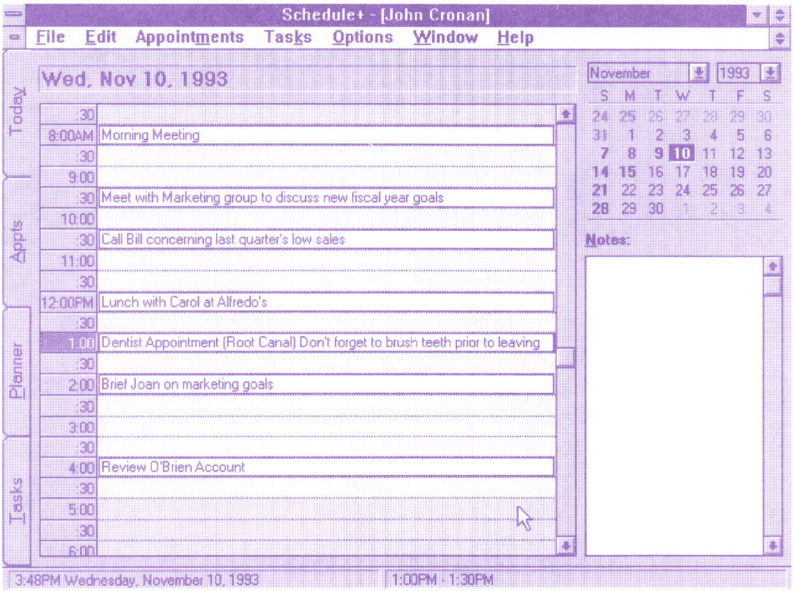

Using Windows for Workgroups' Schedule+ and Other Accessories   **219**

Appointments
to be entered
Figure 8-12.

which is not seen by other users. Your screen should now look like Figure 8-13.

Recurring Appointments

Schedule+ schedules recurring events on any basis you choose. You can set up a new appointment as recurring, or you can designate an existing appointment as recurring from your Appointment Book. The following steps set up the 8:00 a.m. weekly meeting as a recurring appointment:

1. Select the 8:00 a.m. time slot. Open the Appointments menu and choose the New Recurring Appts option. The Recurring Appointment dialog box opens. The box labeled This Appointment Occurs shows the current day of the week and starting date.

Networking Windows for Workgroups

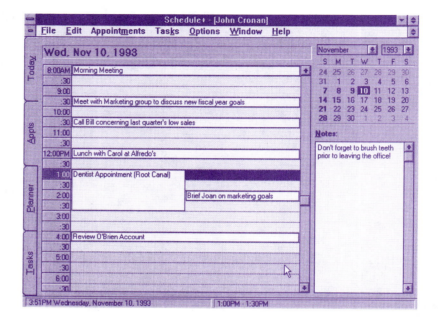

Appointment Book showing multiple entries and a daily note
Figure 8-13.

2. Click on the Change button to open the Change Recurrence dialog box, as shown in Figure 8-14.

   The Change Recurrence dialog box lets you choose the interval between meetings, change the day of the week, establish the duration of the recurrence, and it informs you when the first recurrence will happen.

Change Recurrence dialog box
Figure 8-14.

For this exercise, verify that the Weekly option button is chosen in the area labeled This Occurs, and accept the option in the Every Week On box and the default one-year option in the Duration box.

3. Click on OK to return to the Recurring Appointment dialog box. Leave the Start and Stop times and the Description the same. Click on OK. The weekly meeting time slot is annotated with a recurring appointment icon, as shown here:

You can easily change or delete a recurring appointment with the Edit Recurring Appts command in the Appointments menu.

Adding a Tentative Appointment

Making an appointment tentative shows other users that you are available during that time period. Tentative appointments are handy for scheduling events that can take place in conjunction with other appointments. For example, if you have one appointment of uncertain length, you can schedule another tentative appointment that might overlap. Follow these steps to designate the 10:30 a.m. time slot as a tentative appointment:

1. Select the 10:30 a.m. appointment.
2. Choose the Tentative option from the Appointments menu. The entry now appears in gray. Again, open the Appointments menu. Notice the check mark next to the Tentative option. This option acts as a *toggle*, it's either on or off.

New or existing appointments can also be designated as tentative in the Appointment dialog box. Click on the check box next to Tentative to set up a new appointment or change an existing one.

Setting Reminders

You can use reminders to have Schedule+ notify you of upcoming appointments. Reminders can be set for all appointments (which is the

Schedule+ default you turned off earlier in the General Options dialog box), or they can be set for individual appointments of your choosing. The following steps illustrate how to set an appointment reminder:

1. Look at the present time in the status bar at the bottom of the screen. Choose the next available time slot that is at least 15 minutes from your present time. Select the time slot and type **This is a test of Schedule+ reminders**.

2. Double-click on the time slot to open the Appointment dialog box.

3. Click on the check box next to Set Reminder for, to place an X in the box. The default of 15 minutes before the appointment appears in the box to the right.

4. Press Del and type **5** to shorten the time for the reminder to react. Click on OK.
   Notice the bell icon on the left side of the time slot in the Appointment Book. At the appointed time, a Reminder dialog box appears on your screen and a beep sounds. You can have Schedule+ remind you again of the appointment in a specified period of time or accept the default not to have Schedule+ notify you again.

5. Click on OK to accept the default. You return to the reminder message and the bell is removed from the time slot.

You can set reminders in the Appointment dialog box for new appointments. For existing appointments, you can use the dialog box to change the default settings, as you just did, or you can select the Set Reminder option in the Appointments menu to toggle a reminder on or off. In the latter case, you accept the default of 15 minutes before appointments that is set in the General Options dialog box from the Options menu. You can change the default as you desire. The audible portion of the reminder can also be turned off in the General Options dialog box.

Before filling in your actual appointments, continue with the next section to see how tasks are integrated into your Appointment Book.

Quitting Schedule+

If you need to quit Schedule+, use the Close option in the File menu or the Control menu to temporarily leave Schedule+. The next time you open Schedule+ (assuming your computer remains on) you won't have to sign in. Quitting Schedule+ using the Close and Sign Out option completely signs you out of the program.

Using the Task List

The task list lets you list and manage your longer term tasks. You can view them by priority, due date, or description, or you can organize them into projects. Also, you can set reminders to notify you when a dormant task has become active, you can move completed tasks to your Notes box in the calendar, and you can schedule tasks in your Appointment Book.

Whether you're continuing from the Appointment Book section or are signing into Schedule+ after taking a break, you should be at the current day in your Appointment Book.

Adding Tasks

Adding tasks to your task list is similar to adding appointments to your Appointment Book. If you accept the default settings, tasks can be added directly. For tasks that need modification, you can access a dialog box to effect the changes. Use the following steps to open your task list and begin adding tasks:

1. From your Appointment Book, click on the Tasks tab or press (Alt)-(T). Your blank task list appears, as shown in Figure 8-15.
2. From the Tasks menu, choose the first option, New Task. The Task dialog box opens, as shown here:

3. In the Description text box, type **Form O'Brien Account Team**.

4. Press [Tab] to accept <None> in the Project drop-down list box. This accepts the default, which is no project. Unless you have tasks that are unique to themselves, it is better project management to group your tasks into projects. Type **O'Brien Account** as a project name.

The Due Date default is None. Accepting this keeps the task in your list, but you must remember to do something to it. Using a date for the Due Date lets Schedule+ inform you that some action is required. The By option shows the current date by default, but allows you to change to any desired date.

5. Click on the By option button, and change the date to a week or so in advance of your current date.

The Start Work and Before Due boxes let you set the number of days, weeks, or months in advance of the due date that the task becomes active. In the time before this date, the task is considered inactive and doesn't appear in your list. This is a great advantage for longer term planning, when you don't need to view the task until it's closer to the due

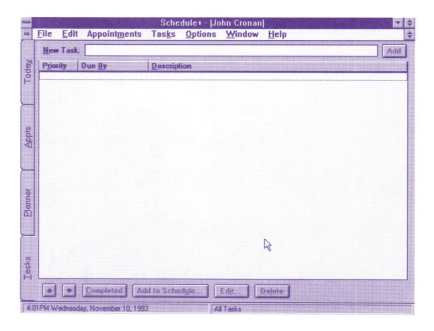

The opening task list screen
Figure 8-15.

Using Windows for Workgroups' Schedule+ and Other Accessories

date. When the Start Work/Before Due date arrives, your task appears in your task list. You can have Schedule+ remind you with a message by clicking on the Set Reminder check box.

6. Accept the 0 default, which makes the task active now.
7. Change the Priority to 1 by selecting the default, 3, and typing **1**, or by clicking the up arrow twice. You can prioritize your tasks from 1 through 9 and then A through Z; 1 being the highest priority, Z the lowest. Leave the Private check box alone for now.
8. Click on OK or press (Enter) to close the dialog box. The task is added to your task list, as shown in Figure 8-16.

Notice the buttons at the bottom of the window. When the project name is selected, only the Edit and Delete buttons are available. Selecting the task allows use of all the buttons.

Another way to enter a task is to use the New Task text box, located below the menu bar. In this case, the task is added to the current project with the Schedule+ default settings. Try adding a task now:

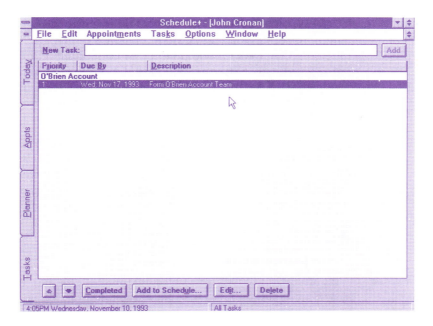

A task entered in the task list
Figure 8-16.

1. Click in the New Task text box. The insertion point appears in the box, letting you know you can enter text. Type **Confirm orders with Ms. O'Brien** and click on the Add button to the right of the text box. The new task is added to the O'Brien Account project, as shown here:

2. Double-click on the task to open the Task dialog box. This is identical to the dialog box used in the previous exercise. Also, you can use the Edit Task option in the Edit menu to display the Task dialog box. You might want to change the priority, due date, or any other parameter. Close the dialog box when finished.

3. Double-click on the project title, "O'Brien Account." The Project dialog box opens, allowing you only to change the project name or restrict its access. Click on OK to return to your task list.

To continue the exercises, you need more projects and tasks in your task list. Before you enter the data, here are a few hints: To create new projects, use the New Project command in the Tasks menu to name them; to set up your tasks, switch between using the Task dialog box and the New Task text box. Don't be concerned if you get a task in the wrong project—either use the Task dialog box to change the name of the project or wait to see how easy it is to move or copy tasks. Finally, notice that the tasks at the top of the task list are not included in a project.

Depending on what date you perform these exercises, the task Due By dates in Figure 8-17 may precede your current date. If so, they will appear in red on your screen. You can increase the year to ensure that all the Due By dates are in the future. Go ahead and practice entering the projects and tasks listed in Figure 8-17 now.

The final task to add is a recurring task. Much like recurring appointments, these tasks happen at a set interval for a specific period. Add a recurring task with the following steps:

Using Windows for Workgroups' Schedule+ and Other Accessories

1. Choose the New Recurring Tasks option from the Tasks menu. The Recurring Task dialog box appears, as shown in Figure 8-18.

2. Type **Conduct monthly account review** in the Description text box and choose the O'Brien Account from the Project drop-down list box.

3. Click on the Change button in the Due By box. In the Change Recurrence dialog box, choose the Monthly option button in the This Occurs option list. The box to the right changes and allows you to specify which day of the month to schedule the task. Choose last Monday.

4. Leave Duration as the default, one year, and click on OK. Returning to the Recurring Task dialog box, change the priority to 2, and click on OK to complete the task and return to the task list. Notice the recurring icon to the left of the task description.

You can edit any recurring task by choosing Edit Recurring Task from the Tasks menu.

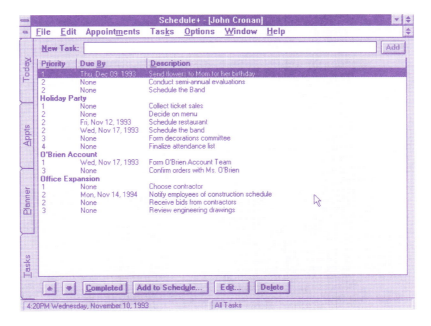

Sample projects and tasks list
Figure 8-17.

Figure 8-18.
Recurring Task dialog box

Modifying Tasks

Now that you have a sizable task list, you can perform a number of actions. You can change the tasks' locations and the order in which they are viewed or sorted, or you can delete unwanted tasks.

Moving and Copying Tasks

The first change to your task list is to make sure the correct tasks are associated with their respective projects. Two of the three tasks at the top of the list are singular tasks and don't belong in a project. The third task, Schedule the Band, should be a part of the Holiday Party. Move this task to its proper project with the steps that follow:

1. Click on the Schedule the Band task and keep the mouse button depressed. Slowly drag the task downward. Notice the mouse pointer now has a task icon attached to it, as shown here:

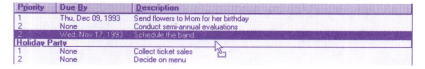

2. Drop the task anywhere in the Holiday Party project. The Schedule the Band task is placed in alphabetical order with the priority-two tasks, and it disappears from its former position. If you have other

Using Windows for Workgroups' Schedule+ and Other Accessories   **229**

tasks that need to be moved, rearrange them now using this drag and drop technique.

You can also copy tasks, which leaves the original task in its time slot and makes an identical copy in another time slot. Just press Ctrl before you drag the task to its new location.

Viewing and Sorting Your Tasks

So far, your tasks have been organized by priority within each project, with the tasks not assigned a project grouped at the beginning of the task list. You can quickly change the order of the tasks by using one of the following four viewing and sorting options available in the Tasks menu:

◆ View by Project (default)

◆ Sort by Priority (default)

◆ Sort by Due Date

◆ Sort by Description

Additionally, you can view just your active tasks, instead of all your tasks, which is the default. See how easy it is to view and sort your tasks with these steps:

1. Open the Tasks menu and click on View by Project to turn it off. Your task list changes to a list of tasks sorted by priority, without showing any project names, as you can see here:

Priority	Due By	Description
1	None	Choose contractor
1	None	Collect ticket sales
1	Wed, Nov 17, 1993	Form O'Brien Account Team
1	Thu, Dec 09, 1993	Send flowers to Mom for her birthday
2	Mon, Nov 29, 1993	Conduct monthly account review
2	None	Conduct semi-annual evaluations
2	None	Decide on menu
2	Mon, Nov 14, 1994	Notify employees of construction schedule
2	None	Receive bids from contractors
2	Fri, Nov 12, 1993	Schedule restaurant
2	Wed, Nov 17, 1993	Schedule the band
3	None	Confirm orders with Ms. O'Brien
3	None	Form decorations committee
3	None	Review engineering drawings
4	None	Finalize attendance list

A quick way to change the priority of any of the listed tasks is to select the task and use the up and down arrows at the bottom of the screen to increase or decrease its priority.

2. Click on the other two sort options to see how they change your list. You can return to View by Project and sort the tasks under the projects in any of the three sort categories. When you are finished experimenting, return your task list to its default View by Project and Sort by Priority settings.

The status bar at the bottom of the screen displays two items of information. On the left side are the current time and date and on the right are the words "All Tasks." All Tasks displays both active and inactive tasks. You can view just your active tasks by selecting the Show Active Tasks option at the bottom of the Tasks menu. Selecting this option turns off All Tasks, and Active Tasks appears in its place. Your task list now shows only tasks that have no due date or those that are in the time frame for you to be working on. Return to the default All Tasks by choosing the Show All Tasks option.

Deleting Tasks

There are two ways to delete tasks from your task list, individually or as part of a deleted project. To delete a single task, select the task and click on the Delete button at the bottom of the screen or press Del. You can also use the Delete Task command in the Edit menu.

Deleting a project is just as easy as deleting a task, but be careful because when you delete a project, you delete all of its associated tasks. If there are any tasks you want to save, move them out of the project you want to delete. This can be done by using the drag and drop method, or you can open each task's Task dialog box and change the project name.

To delete a project, select it and click on the Delete button at the bottom of the screen. A dialog box will warn you that any tasks under that project name also will be deleted. Click on OK when you are sure you are not deleting any useful tasks.

Integrating Tasks with Your Appointment Book

There are two ways you can transfer information from your task list to your Appointment Book and calendar. First, you can move completed tasks to the calendar Notes for the day you completed the task. The task is removed from your task list when you complete a task. Second, you can schedule a task in your Appointment Book. In this case, the task remains in your task list as well as in your Appointment Book. Try both transfer methods with the following steps:

1. Select the first task, Send flowers to Mom for her birthday, and click on the Completed button at the bottom of the screen. The task is removed from your task list.

2. Click on the Today tab to open your Appointment Book. The task is now listed in the Notes box for the current day, as shown here:

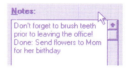

3. Now, return to your task list and select the Collect ticket sales task in the Holiday Party project. Click on the Add to Schedule button at the bottom of the screen. The Choose Time dialog box opens to the current week, as shown in Figure 8-19.

4. You can choose any date for the task to appear in your Appointment Book. Choose a date in the following month and click in the 10:00 a.m. block. Click on OK to close the dialog box.

5. Click on the Appts tab to open your Appointment Book. Figure 8-20 shows the Appointment Book opened with the task now listed as a 10:00 a.m. appointment.

The Schedule+ information stored in your Appointment Book and task list might serve you better if you had a paper copy. The next section shows you how you can print your scheduling data.

232   *Networking Windows for Workgroups*

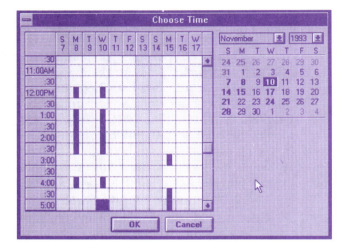

Choose Time dialog box
Figure 8-19.

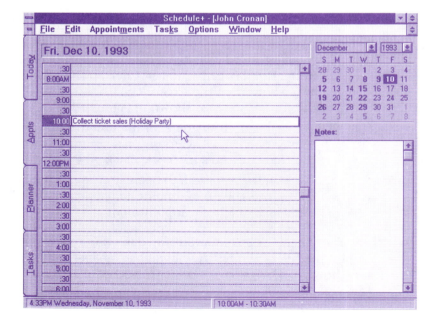

Appointment Book showing an appointment transferred from the task list
Figure 8-20.

Using Windows for Workgroups' Schedule+ and Other Accessories

Printing Your Appointment Book and Task List

You print your Appointment Book the same way that you print your task list with one difference. You can print portions of your Appointment Book (days, weeks, or months). When you print your task list, you have to print the entire list; however, you can choose to print any view and sort. Print your Appointment Book and task list with the following steps:

1. Select the File menu and choose the Print option. The Print dialog box appears, as shown here:

The default Print option is Daily View if you opened the Print dialog box from the Appointment Book; it is Tasks if you came from the Task List. By clicking on the down arrow in the Print drop-down list box, you can choose other options, including printing the Appointment Book by day, week, or month. For this exercise, use the default Daily View to print the Appointment Book by day.

2. In the Starting text box within the Schedule Range area, change the date to the one you used to do the Appointment Book entries at the beginning of this chapter. The 1 and Day(s) in the For box is consistent with Daily View in the Print box.

The type of printer you have determines how much flexibility you have in setting up your printed output. By clicking on the Setup button, you can customize such printing features as page orientation, margins, paper size, and choice of printer. Additional features are available from the Options button. When you have the setup to your liking, return to the Print dialog box.

3. Click on OK to print the Appointment Book data. Your output should look similar to Figure 8-21.
4. To print your task list, first click on the Tasks tab to return to the list. Choose the type of view and sort you want to print.
5. Choose File/Print to open the Print dialog box (the same one you saw printing the Appointment Book). The default Print type is now Tasks. Notice the Schedule Range boxes are dimmed and unavailable.
6. When you have completed the setup, click on OK in the Print dialog box. Your output should look similar to Figure 8-22 if you chose the default, View by Project and Sort by Priority.

Sharing Schedule+

So far, you've been working on your own appointments and tasks. To reap the full potential of Schedule+, you need to access other workgroup members' schedules and let them access yours.

Providing Access to Others

You have several choices for how you let other users access your scheduling data. You can grant the same access privileges to all users, customize privileges to individual users, and classify specific appointments and tasks as private, overriding other access privileges.

1. Choose the Set Access Privileges option from the Options menu. The following dialog box opens:

The Users box identifies the users and their degree of privilege. The default is for all users to have View, which is short for View Free/Busy

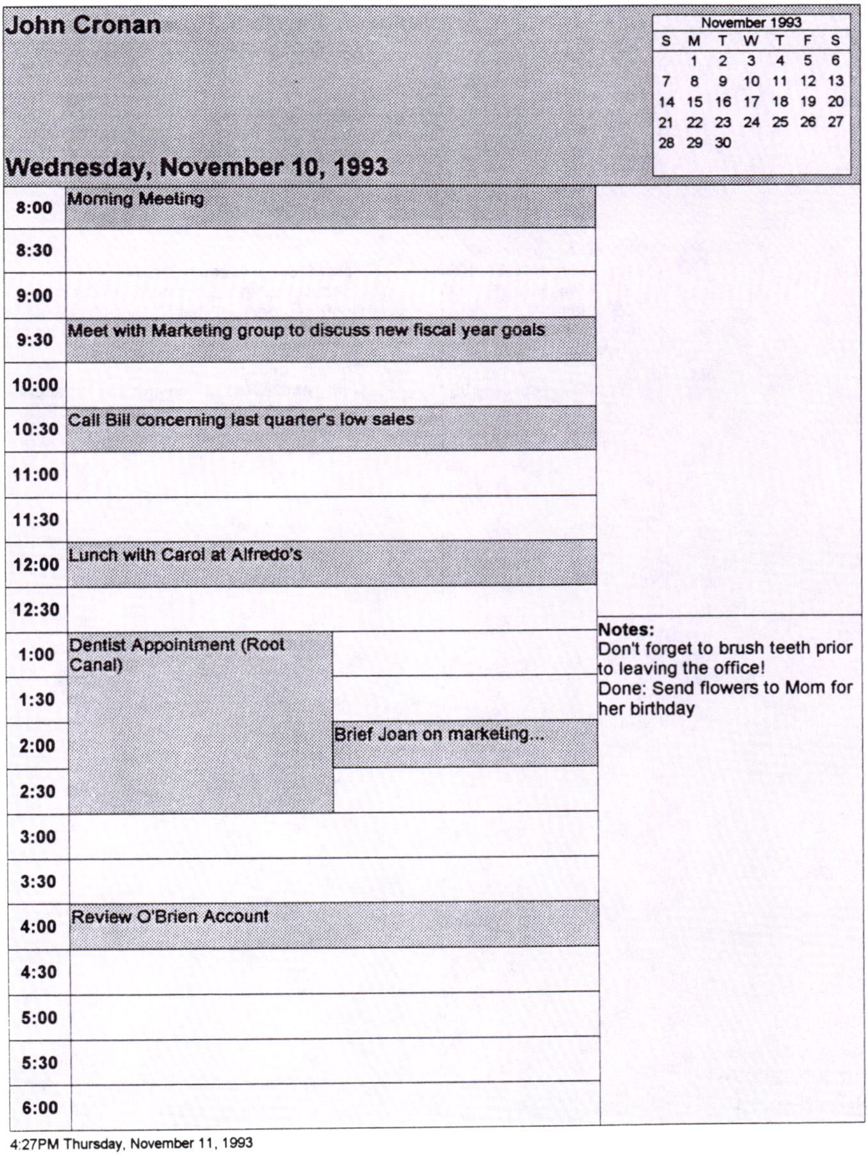

Using Windows for Workgroups' Schedule+ and Other Accessories

John Cronan

			November 1993			
S	M	T	W	T	F	S
	1	2	3	4	5	6
7	8	9	10	11	12	13
14	15	16	17	18	19	20
21	22	23	24	25	26	27
28	29	30				

Wednesday, November 10, 1993

8:00	Morning Meeting
8:30	
9:00	
9:30	Meet with Marketing group to discuss new fiscal year goals
10:00	
10:30	Call Bill concerning last quarter's low sales
11:00	
11:30	
12:00	Lunch with Carol at Alfredo's
12:30	
1:00	Dentist Appointment (Root Canal)
1:30	
2:00	Brief Joan on marketing...
2:30	
3:00	
3:30	
4:00	Review O'Brien Account
4:30	
5:00	
5:30	
6:00	

Notes:
Don't forget to brush teeth prior to leaving the office!
Done: Send flowers to Mom for her birthday

4:27PM Thursday, November 11, 1993

Printed Appointment Book daily view
Figure 8-21.

Networking Windows for Workgroups

Task List as of Thursday, November 11, 1993   **John Cronan**

2	None	Conduct semi-annual evaluations

Holiday Party

1	None	Collect ticket sales
2	None	Decide on menu
2	Fri, Nov 12, 1993	Schedule restaurant
2	Wed, Nov 17, 1993	Schedule the band
3	None	Form decorations committee
4	None	Finalize attendance list

O'Brien Account

1	Wed, Nov 17, 1993	Form O'Brien Account Team
2	Mon, Nov 29, 1993	Conduct monthly account review
3	None	Confirm orders with Ms. O'Brien

Office Expansion

1	None	Choose contractor
2	Mon, Nov 14, 1994	Notify employees of construction schedule
2	None	Receive bids from contractors
3	None	Review engineering diagrams

4:11 PM Thursday, November 11, 1993

Printed task list
Figure 8-22.

Times. You can change this, choosing from a range of privileges—None to Modify—which applies to all users.

There are probably users in your workgroup who you want to have more privileges than others.

2. Click on the Add button. An Add User dialog box opens that allows you to select members of your workgroup for specific privileges.
3. Select some users to have specific privileges. Click on the Add button to include them in your Users list. Click on OK to return to the Set Access Privileges dialog box.
4. Assign each user his or her specific privilege. When you are done, your Users list looks similar to this:

The last privilege, Assistant, is discussed in the section, "Using Schedule+ to Arrange Meetings," later in this chapter.

Gaining Access to Other Users' Schedules

Just as you let other users access your data, you can access their schedules, depending on what privileges they have assigned you. The following steps show how easy it is to access other users' data:

1. Open the File menu and choose the Open Other's Appt. Book option. The Open Other's Appt. Book dialog box opens with the users in your workgroup listed.
2. Select the user whose Appointment Book you want to access, and click on OK.

If you have the proper access privilege, his or her Appointment Book will appear on your screen. You can also access the task list by clicking on the Tasks tab. Schedule+ will inform you if the other user's Appointment Book is unavailable or if you don't have access.

You maneuver through someone else's Appointment Book or task list the same way you do in yours, except you might not have full privileges. When you have finished touring the schedule, close the Appointment Book by double-clicking on the Control menu box, or choose Close from the Control menu.

Using Other Scheduling Programs

Your scheduling information can be shared with similar programs, such as Windows 3.0 Calendar and WordPerfect Office. Additionally, you can copy the information from these other programs to your Appointment Book. Finally, if you work offline, the Schedule+ data file can be copied to a floppy disk so you can work on your schedule at home or on a portable computer.

The exercises in this section do not need to be worked through unless you want to copy or merge your scheduling files at this time. You'll probably just want to follow along for future use.

To copy your Schedule+ information to another file or floppy disk, use the following steps:

1. Choose the Export Appointments option from the File menu to display the following dialog box:

2. Click on the arrow on the File Format drop-down list box to reveal the two available file formats that Schedule+ can copy to: Schedule+ and Text.

Using Windows for Workgroups' Schedule+ and Other Accessories

If you are copying to a floppy disk to use your scheduling information offline, select the Schedule+ format. The file extension is .SCH. Data copied for use in other scheduling programs should use the Text format, which appears with a .TXT extension. The last format you used will be the default for future exports, so be sure to check which format is active before you export.

3. Choose a Schedule Range. Leave the default, All, or select your own range in the From and To text boxes. Choose whether you want to include your Notes and then click on OK. A different Export Appointments dialog box opens, where you can select or type the drive, directory, and filename for your exported file. Click on OK when you have finished.

To import scheduling data from your offline work or from other programs, follow these steps:

1. Open the File Import Appointments dialog box and select or type the drive, directory, and filename for your imported file. Click on OK when you have finished. The Import Format dialog box opens, as shown here:

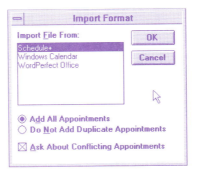

2. Select the file format you're copying from in the Import File From list box.
3. Choose Add All Appointments or Do Not Add Duplicate Appointments, and whether you want to be prompted prior to copying conflicting appointments. Click on OK when finished.

Networking Windows for Workgroups

Using Schedule+ to Arrange Meetings

One of the major features of Schedule+ is group scheduling. From your computer, you can quickly compare the schedules of other workgroup members to your own and then schedule a mutually acceptable meeting. Verification messages can then be sent and responded to. To help you manage your own, and the workgroup's, schedules, you can assign an Assistant. An Assistant has access privileges above other users. Finally, you can schedule the availability of workgroup resources, such as conference rooms, in addition to the people who use them.

Learn how to use the Planner and your Appointment Book to schedule meetings in the steps that follow.

1. Click on the Planner tab at the left of your screen. The Planner opens, showing a matrix of your schedule. Figure 8-23 illustrates a typical Planner page.

2. If the users you want to attend the meeting are not listed in the Attendees box, click on Change to add them. The Select Attendees dialog box opens, allowing you to add users from any of your Mail

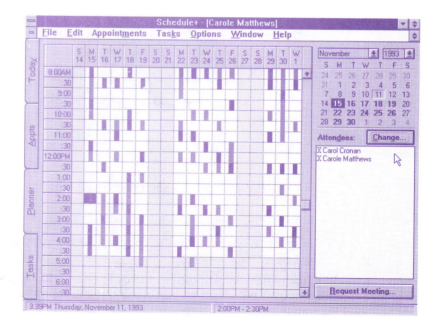

A typical Planner
Figure 8-23.

Using Windows for Workgroups' Schedule+ and Other Accessories

address lists. Click on OK when you have identified all the participants in your meeting.

3. Click on a time slot that is open for all users. Next, click on the Request Meeting button to display the Send Request dialog box, as shown in Figure 8-24.

4. Type in a subject, decide whether you want response messages, and type in any message text. When you are finished, click on the Send button to transmit the meeting request. The meeting appears in your Appointment Book. Notice the meeting icon to the left of the time slot's subject.

You can also schedule meetings from your Appointment Book by using these steps:

1. From the Appointments menu, open the Appointment dialog box. Click on the Choose Time button. A minimized window of your Planner appears. Assign your meeting participants now, or use the Invite button from the Appointment dialog box when you return to it. Select a time everyone is free, or use Auto-Pick to find an open time slot for you. Click on OK when finished. You are returned to the Appointment dialog box.

2. Type a description of the meeting in the Description text box. This description will appear in the Appointment Book's time slots. Click on OK. The Send Request dialog box opens.

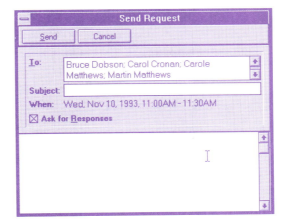

Send Request dialog box
Figure 8-24.

3. Type in a subject, decide whether you want response messages, and type in any message text. When you are finished, click on the Send button to transmit the meeting request. Notice the meeting icon to the left of the time slot's subject.

If you asked for responses to your meeting requests, they appear in your Schedule+ Message window, as well as your Mail Inbox. You can respond to them from the Schedule+ Message window or from Mail.

Once a meeting is scheduled, it is very easy to reschedule or cancel. (It might not be quite as easy to deal with your co-workers!) To change a scheduled meeting, follow these steps:

1. From your Appointment Book, move the meeting to the new time slot by using drag and drop or the Edit menu command, Move Appt.

2. A dialog box appears asking if you want to notify the meeting attendees of the change. Choose Yes.

3. The Send Request dialog box appears, as it did for your initial request. Fill it out and click on OK.

To cancel a meeting, these are the steps to use:

1. Select the meeting in your Appointment Book.

2. Choose Delete Appt from the Edit menu. A dialog box appears asking if you want to notify the meeting attendees of the change. Choose Yes. A Cancel Meeting dialog box appears.

3. Type in a message, if you desire. Click on the Send button when you are finished.

Using an Assistant

You can designate an Assistant to access your Schedule+ information and conduct business for you. The Assistant can perform the same actions in your Appointment Book that you do. The major difference is that when your Assistant communicates to other users, they are notified that the Assistant is acting on your behalf.

To set up a user as your Assistant, follow these steps:

Using Windows for Workgroups' Schedule+ and Other Accessories   **243**

1. Choose the Set Access Privileges dialog box from the Options menu.
2. Select the user you want to be your Assistant. If the user's name is not in the Users box, add him or her with the Add button and subsequent dialog box.
3. Choose the Assistant option in the Privileges box. Click on OK.

If you are someone else's Assistant, use the following steps to access their Appointment Book:

1. Choose the Open Other's Appt Book option in the File menu. Select the user whose Assistant you will be (you can be the Assistant to more than one user).
2. Click on OK. The other Appointment Book appears on your screen.

You can view or change the other person's schedule and schedule meetings on his or her behalf. You receive any responses to meeting requests that you send, and you respond to requests for meetings from the other workgroup users. The other person's schedule is automatically updated.

Scheduling Resources

A *resource* is a tangible commodity that is scheduled, for example, conference and training rooms, overhead projectors, and company vehicles. Like another user, the resource must have a Mail account. Before you can set up a resource, make sure your workgroup administrator has established the account.

Set up a resource with the following steps:

1. Close Schedule+ (if you have it running), using the Close and Sign Out option. Sign back into Schedule+ using the name and password for the resource.
2. Choose General Options from the Options menu. Click on the check box next to This Account is for a Resource, to place an X in the box, and then click on OK.
3. Again, in the Options menu, choose Set Access Privileges.

All users should at least have View privileges. In order for users to schedule resource times directly, they need to have Create privileges. Depending on the size of your workgroup, you might consider appointing a resource Assistant to have sole control in managing the resource.

4. When you've decided how the resource is to be used, select the applicable privilege level, and then click on OK to complete the resource setup.

The remainder of the chapter discusses three accessories, Chat, Net Watcher, and WinMeter. You can use these accessories to take part in computer "conversations" and to see how your computer resources are being used by you and others.

Using Chat

Chat allows you to communicate with other users in your workgroup by typing what you want to say and having your words appear on their screens. This is a handy feature when you need to contact someone who is constantly on the telephone. The simplest way to learn Chat is to just start using it:

1. Open the Program Manager's Accessories group and double-click on the Chat icon. The Chat window opens, as shown in Figure 8-25.
2. Maximize the window by double-clicking anywhere in the colored portion of the title bar.

Notice the three tools below the Conversation menu. They allow you to "Dial" (initiate communications with another computer), to Answer an incoming call, and to Hang Up or end a call. Knowing the use of these tools, or their corresponding commands in the Conversation menu, is all there really is to using Chat. The leftmost icon is Dial.

3. To initiate a call, click on Dial to open the Select Computer dialog box, as shown in Figure 8-26.
4. Select the computer name of the user you want to chat with and click on OK. A message will appear in the status bar, at the bottom of the Chat window, letting you know your call has been answered.

Using Windows for Workgroups' Schedule+ and Other Accessories

Chat window
Figure 8-25.

When your call is answered, start typing your message in the upper editing window. You can change the windows from the top and bottom configuration to side-by-side with the Preferences option in the Options menu. Once you change them they stay changed.

The person you are calling can answer at the same time you continue to type your message. The message appears in the lower window, as shown in Figure 8-27.

To end a call, click on Hang Up, the rightmost icon. If the person you were chatting with hangs up before you do, you'll receive a message to that effect in the status bar.

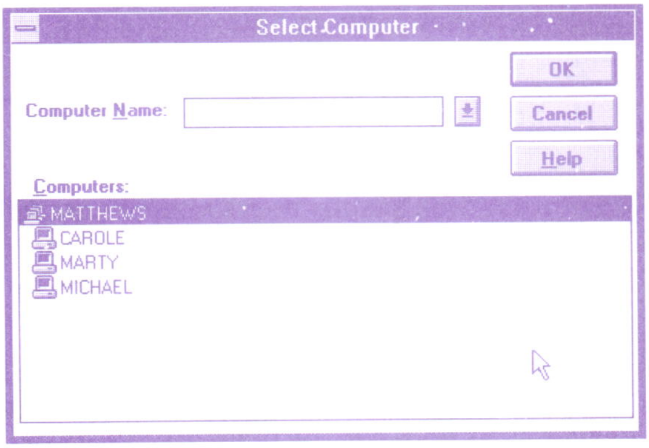

Select Computer dialog box
Figure 8-26.

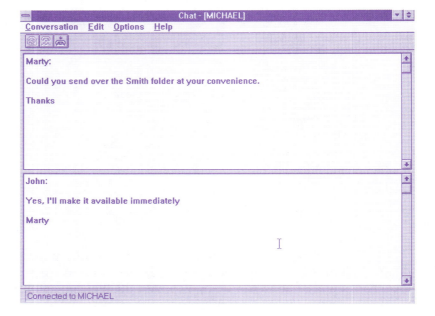

Chat window with an outgoing and incoming message
Figure 8-27.

How you receive a call depends on whether you have Chat running. If Chat is running when the call comes through, you'll hear a beep, and a message appears in the status bar. If Chat isn't running, the Chat icon appears on your screen. To answer the call:

1. Open the Chat window, if it isn't already, by double-clicking on the Chat icon.
2. Click on Answer, the middle toolbar icon.
3. Start typing your message.

Through the Options menu you can change the setup in your Chat window. You can change your typing font and the font of received messages; the background color of the Chat window; and whether the toolbar, status bar, and speaker are turned on or off.

Also, you can choose to have Chat remain in the foreground by turning on the Always On Top option in the Control menu. And remember, Chat Help is always available to answer your questions.

Using Windows for Workgroups' Schedule+ and Other Accessories

4. Close Chat by double-clicking on the Control menu box or choosing Close from the Control menu.

Net Watcher

Net Watcher allows you to see who is connected to your computer and which of your shared resources are being used. It also gives you the opportunity to disconnect users from your resources. You must be running Windows for Workgroups in 386 enhanced mode for Net Watcher to operate.

Use the following steps to see how Net Watcher works:

1. Open the Program Manager's Accessories group. Double-click on the Net Watcher icon. Net Watcher opens, as shown in Figure 8-28.

Net Watcher is divided into two windows: the left side displays the computer names of users connected to your computer, and the right side shows which of your resources a selected user is currently using.

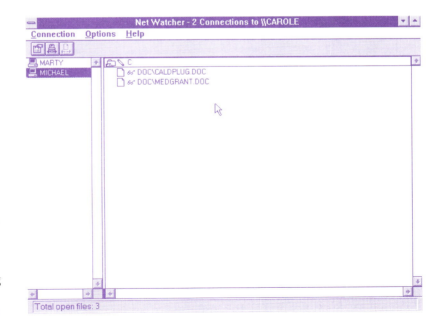

Net Watcher's opening screen showing resource sharing
Figure 8-28.

2. To better see how Net Watcher works on your computer, have at least one member of your workgroup connect to one of your shared directories, and open a file.

3. Select a connected user listed in the left window. Notice the icon next to the resource he or she is using. A pencil icon means you have given that user write permission; read permission is indicated by a pair of eyeglasses.

In the toolbar you'll see three tools. Properties tells you about the selected user, Disconnect disconnects the selected user, and Close File closes the file opened by the selected user.

4. Click on the leftmost of the three tools or select the Connections menu and choose Properties to see more information about the connected user, as shown here:

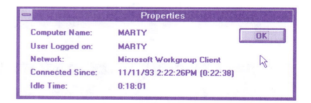

In addition to viewing the listed information, you can disconnect a user from the file they have open, or disconnect them completely from your computer. The rightmost tool, or the Connection Close option in the File menu, is used to disconnect someone from an individual file. Use the center tool, or the Disconnect command from the Connection menu, to perform a total disconnect.

CAUTION: Be aware that disconnecting a user from one of your files or your computer can cause the loss of any unsaved data.

5. Click on OK to close the Properties dialog box.

Using Windows for Workgroups' Schedule+ and Other Accessories

Net Watcher updates the information on connected users every 20 seconds. If you want an instant update, choose Refresh from the Options menu. The Options menu also lets you adjust the sizes of the two windows, and turn the toolbar and status bar off or on. As with Schedule+ and Chat, Net Watcher provides its own help facility to assist you when needed.

6. Close Net Watcher by double-clicking on the Control menu box or choosing Close from the Control menu.

WinMeter

WinMeter graphically displays the percentage of your CPU's time that is dedicated to your computer, and the percentage that is being used to support connected users—acting as a *server*. As with Net Watcher, you must be running Windows for Workgroups in 386 enhanced mode for WinMeter to operate.

Follow these steps to see how WinMeter measures your CPU's performance:

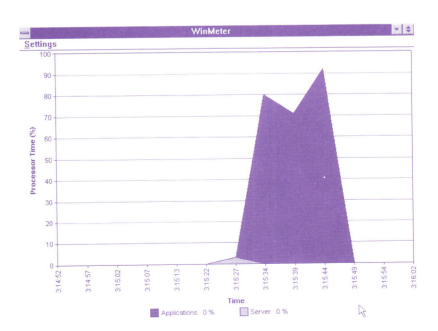

WinMeter showing CPU usage
Figure 8-29.

1. Open the Program Manager's Accessories group. Double-click on the WinMeter icon. WinMeter opens, as shown in Figure 8-29.

In this instance, WinMeter is showing a high application use (the upper portion of the curve) against low server use (the small triangle at the bottom of the curve). Processor time is measured along the vertical axis and elapsed time is shown along the horizontal axis.

2. Open the Settings menu.

You can choose the interval rate at which WinMeter measures elapsed time, the colors that are used to show application use versus server use, and whether you want the graph legend and title bar displayed.

3. Close WinMeter by double-clicking on the Control menu box or choosing Close from the Control menu.

INDEX

Numbers and Symbols

8–bit network interface cards, 68–69, 70

16–bit network interface cards, 68–69, 70, 72

286 computers, 143–144

386 Enhanced function, 48

386 enhanced mode
  Net Watcher and, 247
  sharing resources in, 120
  versus standard mode, 95–96
  system requirements for, 85
  troubleshooting, 110–111
  WinMeter and, 249

$ (dollar sign), in filename extensions, 148

– (hyphen)
  in computer names, 100
  opening Control menu with, 42

_ (underscore character), 100, 115

\ (backslash), in pathnames, 159, 171

A

About option, Help system, 56

Access privileges
  changing, 128–129, 134–135, 140, 141
  to ClipBook pages, 138–140
  to directories, 124–125, 128–129, 148–149
  full access, 120, 124–125, 139
  to others' schedules, 237–238
  to printers, 131–132, 134–135
  read–only access, 120, 124–125, 139
  shared resources and, 120
  to your schedule, 234–237
  See also Passwords

Accessories, 20–22
  See also Chat; Net Watcher; WinMeter

Accessories window, 33–37

Active windows, 24, 135

Adapters. *See* Network interface cards

Address Book

251

Personal, 175, 176–177
Postoffice List, 174–176, 186
Address groups, 178, 185–186
Address settings
 base I/O port, 72–74
 base memory, 74–76
Administrator Account dialog box, 194
 See also Workgroup Postoffice administrator
Alt key
 + F4 key (exit), 57, 133
 + H (Help), 55
 + hyphen (opening Control menu), 42
 + Prt Sc key (copying active windows), 135
 + Backspace (opening Control menu), 43
 for menu functions, 42
Application icons, 23–24
 of inactive programs, 37
 moving, 29, 37
Application windows, 22–23, 28–29
Applications
 cutting and copying from, 135–136
 exiting, 57
 starting, 33–37, 86
 starting automatically, 96–97
 See also Main group applications
Appointment Book. *See* Schedule+ Appointment Book
Appointment dialog box, 214–217, 222, 241
Appointment software, 10–11
 Schedule+ and, 238–241
ARCnet cards, 69–70, 75
Arrow keys, 42
Assistant user, for Appointment Book, 242–243

Attach dialog box, Mail, 190
AUTOEXEC.BAT file
 setup changes to, 87, 88–89
 troubleshooting, 104

B

Backing up, 8, 198–199
Backslash (\), 159
Base I/O port address settings, 72–74
Base memory address settings, 74–76
BNC connectors, 65
Boards. *See* Network interface cards
Bus topology, 14, 64–65
Buses, network cards and, 68–69

C

Cables, 65–68
 ARCnet cards and, 70
 coaxial, 65–66, 69
 Ethernet cards and, 69
 installing, 78
 network design and, 63
 purchasing, 77
 telephone, 67
 topologies and, 14–15
 troubleshooting, 81, 103
 twisted-pair, 66–68, 69
Calendaring software, 10–11
 Schedule+ and, 238–241
Cards. *See* Network interface cards
Cascading menus, 38
CD-ROM drives, 9, 113
Change Recurrence dialog box, 220, 227–228
Chat application, 244–247
 See also Mail application

Index

Choose Time dialog box, 231, 232
Client workstations, 4–5, 12
   See also Workstations
Client–server LANs
   overview of, 4–5
   versus peer–to–peer LANs, 6–7,
      12–13, 17
Client–server operating systems, 16
Clipboard
   versus ClipBook Viewer, 20, 52, 55,
      135, 156–157
   cutting/copying to from
      applications, 135–136
   pasting to ClipBook from, 136–139
ClipBook, 135–139
   access privileges to, 138–139
   changing access to, 140
   ClipBook Viewer and, 135, 157
   connecting to, 158–160
   disconnecting from, 160
   displaying users of, 125–127
   enabling/disabling sharing, 100, 141
   naming pages, 138
   object linking and embedding from,
      160–162
   pasting from, 160–161
   pasting from Clipboard into,
      136–139
   sharing pages of, 137–139
ClipBook Viewer
   Clipboard and, 20, 52, 55, 135,
      156–157
   ClipBook and, 135, 157
   object linking and embedding with,
      160–162
   overview of, 47, 156–158
   toolbar, 157–158
   using, 52–55
ClipBook Viewer window, 136–137

Close Files button, 128
Close option, Control menu, 43
Coaxial cables, 65–66
   ARCnet cards and, 70
   Ethernet cards and, 69
   versus twisted–pair cables, 68
Color function, Control Panel, 48
Comments, for computer name, 100
Compressed files, on Setup disks, 115
Compressing, mail files, 198
Computer Name text box, 159
Computers
   286, 143–144
   enabling sharing of, 100
   lockups, 106–107
   modes and, 96, 143–144
   naming, 99–100
   Performance Priority setting, 100
   servers, 4, 7, 12
   types of network, 11–13
   WinMeter and, 249–250
   See also 386 enhanced mode;
      Hardware; Standard mode;
      Workstations
CONFIG.SYS file
   LASTDRIVE command and, 144–145
   setup changes to, 87, 88, 89
   troubleshooting, 104
Conflicts, device, 79–81
Connect Network Drive dialog box
   features of, 146–149
   troubleshooting, 112–113
Connect Network Printer dialog box
   features of, 150–154, 155–156
   troubleshooting, 112–113
Connectors, 65–66, 67, 77
Contents option, Help system, 56
Control menu, 23, 43–46, 136
Control menu box, 23

Control Panel, 47–50
Copy option, Control menu, 44
Copying
   from applications, 135–136
   ClipBook pages, 160–162
   files from Setup disks, 115–116
   tasks, 228–229
Create Directory dialog box, 52
Create Workgroup Postoffice dialog
   box, 194
Ctrl key
   + C (copy), 53
   + V (paste), 53
   selecting files with, 51
Custom Setup, 91–93
Cutting, from applications, 135–136

D

Daisy–chaining. *See* Bus topology
Databases, shared, 10
Date/Time function, Control Panel, 48
Decompressing files, on Setup disks,
   115
Deleted Mail folder, 187
Desktop, 23
Desktop function, Control Panel, 48
Desktop utilities, 11
Device drivers. *See* Drivers
Devices
   IRQ settings, 73
   network card conflicts with, 79–81
   port address settings, 74
Diagnostic programs, 79, 80, 104
Dialog boxes, 39–41, 42
DIP switches, 71–72
Directories
   access privileges to, 124–125
   browsing, 145, 147

changing access to, 128–129
connecting to, 145–149
creating, 52
disconnecting from, 149
displaying users of, 125–127
enabling/disabling sharing, 100, 141
file management in, 50–51
naming, 123, 148, 171
network drives and, 144, 146–147
passwords for, 124–125, 148–149
pathnames for, 121, 147
root, 121, 144
setup and, 88–89
sharing, 122–125
sharing at startup, 132, 148
stopping sharing, 129
Disconnect command, 160
Disconnect Network Drive command,
   149
Disconnect Network Printer
   command, 156
Disk space, requirements for, 85
Disk–caching programs, 88, 108
Diskless workstations, 104
Display adapters, 62–63, 85
Distributed processing, 4
Document windows, 22–23, 28–29
Documents
   destination, 161
   opening with applications, 97
   printing, 133–134
   source, 161
Dollar sign ($), 148
DOS. *See* MS–DOS
Double–backslashes (\\), 159, 171
Drivers
   defined, 87
   network interface card, 72–74
   setup and, 88

Index

troubleshooting, 108
Drivers function, Control Panel, 49
Drives, network
    connecting to, 146–149
    disconnecting from, 149
    reserving drive letters, 144–145
    shared directories and, 144

E

Edit option, Control menu, 44
8–bit network interface cards, 68–69, 70
EISA buses, 68–69
Electronic mail software, 11
    See also Mail application
Embedding
    ClipBook pages, 160–162
    in mail, 191–192
EMM386 memory manager, 75–76, 80
Enable Sharing check box, 100
Encrypting, e–mail and, 11
Enter key, 42
Enter Network Password dialog box, 149
Enter Your Account Details dialog box, 172
Esc key, 42
EtherExpress 16 network card, 106
Ethernet cables, 69
Ethernet cards, 69, 75
Exiting. *See* Quitting
EXPAND command, 115–116
Expanded memory. *See* Memory
Expansion slots, 68
Export Appointments dialog box, 238–239
Express Setup, 90–91, 93

F

F1 key, for Help, 55
F3 key, quitting Setup program, 93
F4 key, exiting, 57, 133
F10 key, for menu functions, 42
FastTips service, 116
Fax boards, 8, 85
File Import Appointments dialog box, 239
File Manager, 47, 50–52
    browsing shared directories, 145, 147
    closing files, 128
    Connect Network Drive command, 112, 146
    connecting to shared directories, 145–149
    displaying users, 125–127
    Network Properties dialog box, 127, 128
    Open Files dialog box, 126–127, 128
    sending mail from, 179
    sharing directories, 122–125
    Stop Sharing Directory dialog box, 129
File menu, Program Manager, 38–39
File servers, 4, 7, 12
Filename extensions
    for compressed files, 115
    dollar sign ($) in, 148
    for exported appointment files, 239
Files
    attaching to mail, 189–191
    closing, 128
    displaying users of, 125–127
    managing, 50–52
    naming, 148
Floppy drives, 84, 108
Folder Properties dialog box, 184

Folders, mail, 183–184
Fonts function, Control Panel, 48
Full access, 120, 124–125, 139

G

General Options dialog box,
  Schedule+, 213
Go To Date dialog box, 217–218
Group icons, 23
Groups, address, 178, 185–186
Groupware, 3, 10–11

H

Hard drives, 8, 62, 85
Hardware, 7–9
  CD–ROM drives, 9, 113
  connectors, 65–66, 67, 77
  floppy drives, 84, 108
  installing, 78–79
  modems and fax boards, 8, 85
  purchasing, 77–78
  requirements, 13, 84–85
  terminators, 64, 77, 103
  troubleshooting, 79–81, 103–106
  See also Cables; Computers; Mouse;
    Network interface cards;
    Printers; Troubleshooting
Hardware Compatibility List, 84, 85
Help system, 55–57
  Mail, 167–169
  Schedule+, 209–211
Hexadecimal notation, 73
Highlighting objects, 24
Hubs, 14–15, 64, 77
Hyphen (–), 42

I

I/O port address settings, 72–74
I–beam pointer, 36
Icons
  for Accessories, 21
  application, 23–24
  group, 23
  Mail, 170
  program–item, 86
Import Format dialog box, 239
Importing appointments, 238–239
Inboxes, Mail, 167, 168, 173, 174
Insertion point, 36
Installing
  cables, 78
  hardware, 78–79
  network interface cards, 78–79
  network printers, 154–156
  Windows for Workgroups, 93–95
Intel EtherExpress 16 network card,
  106
Interface cards. See Network interface
  cards
International function, 48
IRQ settings, 72, 73
ISA buses, 68–69

J

Jumpers, network interface card,
  71–72, 80

K

Keyboard function, Control Panel, 48
Keyboard shortcuts. See Shortcut keys

Index

L

LAN cards. *See* Network interface cards
LAN Manager, Microsoft, 101, 201
LAN software, 9–10
   See also Software
LANs (Local Area Networks). *See*
   Networks
LASTDRIVE command, 144–145
Licensing agreements, 9, 10
Linking, ClipBook pages, 160–162
Local ClipBook. *See* ClipBook
Logging on, 97–98
Logon Settings dialog box, 101
LPT ports, 150, 151–152

M

Mail application, 47, 165–202
   Address Book, 174–177
   address groups, 178, 185–186
   attaching files to mail, 189–191
   deleting mail, 187
   e–mail explained, 11
   embedding in, 191–192
   entering mail, 177–178
   filing mail, 183–184
   finding mail, 186–187
   folders in, 183–184
   forwarding mail, 181–183
   Help, 167–169
   Inboxes, 167, 168, 173, 174
   Microsoft LAN Manager and, 201
   modifying user accounts, 196–197
   Novell NetWare and, 201
   offline use of, 189
   other networks and, 200–201
   Personal Address Book, 175,
      176–177

   personal mailboxes, 167, 168,
      172–174
   Postoffice List, 174–176, 186
   printing mail, 188
   quitting, 188
   receiving mail, 179–180
   replying to mail, 180–181
   Schedule+ and, 208–209, 211–212
   sending mail, 177–179
   signing in, 173–174
   starting for first time, 169–170
   templates, 188–189
   troubleshooting, 201–202
   versus Workgroup Postoffice, 193
   See also Chat application;
      Workgroup Postoffice;
      Workgroup Postoffice
      administrator
Mail Sign In dialog box, 173, 211–212
Mailboxes. *See* Personal mailboxes
Main group applications, 46–55
   ClipBook Viewer, 52–55
   Control Panel, 47–50
   File Manager, 50–52
   icons for, 23–24
   overview of, 46–47
Mark option, Control menu, 44, 136
Maximize button, 23, 29
Maximize option, Control menu, 43
MCA buses, 68–69
Meetings, scheduling, 208–209,
   240–242
Memory
   network design and, 61–62
   requirements for, 85
   and reserving drive letters, 144–145
   upper, 76
   virtual, 95
Memory address settings, 74–76

Memory managers
    base memory address settings and, 75–76
    hardware problems and, 80
    setup and, 89
Memory-resident software
    peer-to-peer LANs and, 6–7
    setup and, 93
    troubleshooting, 109
Menu bar, 23
Menus, 38–39, 42
Message Finder dialog box, 186–187
Messages. *See* Mail application
Microsoft Diagnostics (MSD) program, 104, 105
Microsoft LAN Manager, 101, 201
Microsoft Product Support Services, 116–117
Microsoft Windows for Workgroups
    clients and servers and, 13
    Control menu, 23, 43–46, 136
    Control Panel, 47–50
    customizing Network settings, 99–101
    dialog boxes, 39–41
    features of, 10–11
    Hardware Compatibility List, 84, 85
    Help system, 55–57
    installing, 93–95
    logging on, 97–98
    menus, 38–39
    modes, 95–96
    mouse operation in, 24–28
    network interface card settings and, 106
    overview of, 19–22
    peer-to-peer LANs and, 6
    as a peer-to-peer operating system, 17
    quitting, 57
    scroll bars, 31–33
    starting, 95–98
    starting applications, 33–37, 86, 96–97
    startup screen, 22–24
    system requirements, 13, 84–85
    technical support, 116–117
    topologies for, 65
    tutorial option, 56, 94–95
    upgrading from Windows 3.0 to 3.1, 87–88
    windows in, 28–31
    See also File Manager; Print Manager; Program Manager; Setup program; Troubleshooting
Minimize button, 23, 29
Minimize option, Control menu, 43
Modems, 8, 85
Monitors, 62–63, 85
Mouse
    operation of, 24–28
    requirements for, 85
    troubleshooting, 114–115
Mouse function, Control Panel, 48, 49–50
Mouse pointer, 24, 36
Move option, Control menu, 43
MSD (Microsoft Diagnostics) program, 104, 105
MS-DOS, 76, 84, 102
MS-DOS Prompt application, 47
MSMAIL.INI file, 198–199
MSMAIL.MMF file, 189, 198–199
Multiuser systems, 3–4

Name Finder dialog box, 175

Index

Naming
  ClipBook pages, 138
  computers, 99–100
  personal mailboxes, 173
  shared directories, 123, 148, 171
  shared printers, 131, 148
  See also Filename extensions
Net Watcher application, 125, 133, 247–249
NetWare, 101, 201
Network adapter driver, 105
Network cables. *See* Cables
Network Disk Resources dialog box, 170, 171–172
Network drives. *See* Drives
Network function, Control Panel, 48, 99–101
Network hardware. *See* Hardware
Network interface cards, 68–70
  8-bit and 16-bit, 68–69
  ARCnet cards, 68, 69–70, 75
  base I/O port address settings, 72–74
  base memory address settings, 74–76
  device conflicts with, 79–81
  diagnostic utility, 79, 80, 104
  drivers for, 72–74
  Ethernet cards, 68, 69, 75
  expansion slots and, 68
  handling, 70
  installing, 78–79
  IRQ settings, 72, 73
  jumpers and switches, 70–72, 81
  network design and, 63
  node address setting, 76
  overview of, 13–14, 68
  protocols for, 68
  purchasing, 77
  requirements for, 85
  settings, 70–77, 81

  troubleshooting, 79–81, 103–106
Network operating systems, 16–17
  See also Software
Network printers. *See* Printers
Network Properties dialog box, 127, 128
Network Settings dialog box, 99–101
Networks, 1–17
  benefits of, 7–11
  defined, 2–4
  designing, 60–64
  hardware requirements, 77–78
  versus multiuser systems, 3–4
  parts of, 11–17
  types of, 3–7
  See also Client–server LANs; Peer-to-peer LANs
New Folder dialog box, 183–184
New Group dialog box, 185–186
Next option, Control menu, 44
Node address setting, 76
Nodes, 6, 14–15
  See also Peer-to-peer LANs
Notepad application, 102
Novell NetWare, 101, 201

O

Object linking and embedding (OLE)
  ClipBook pages, 160–162
  embedding objects in mail, 191–192
Open Directory dialog box, 175, 176
Open Files dialog box, 126–127, 128
Open Others' Appt. Book dialog box, 237–238
Operating systems, 6–7
  See also Software
Outboxes, Mail, 167

P

Parallel ports, assigning to shared
    printers, 150, 151–152
Passwords
    for ClipBook pages, 139
    deleting, 112
    for directories, 124–125, 148–149
    forgotten, 112, 202
    full access, 125, 139
    logging on with, 97–98
    for personal mailboxes, 173–174
    for Postoffice administrator, 194
    for printers, 131–132
    read–only, 125, 139
    resource sharing and, 120
    See also Access privileges
Paste dialog box, 53–54, 137
Paste option, Control menu, 44
Pasting
    from Clipboard into ClipBook,
        136–139
    ClipBook pages, 160–162
Pathnames
    backslash (\) in, 159
    for network printers, 121, 152
    for shared directories, 121, 147
    for Workgroup Postoffice, 171
Peer–to–peer LANs
    versus client–server LANs, 6–7,
        12–13, 17
    overview of, 6–7
    servers in, 7
Peer–to–peer operating systems, 17
Peer–to–peer workstations, 12–13
Performance Priority option, 100
Personal Address Book, 176–177
    address groups, 185–186
    See also Address Book
Personal Groups dialog box, 185–186

Personal mailboxes, 167, 168
    opening, 172–173
    passwords for, 173–174
PIF Editor, 47
PIF files, 86
Planner. *See* Schedule+ Planner
Pointers, 24, 36
Ports
    address settings for, 72–74
    assigning to shared printers, 150,
        151–152
Ports function, Control Panel, 48
Postoffice administrator. *See*
    Workgroup Postoffice
    administrator
Postoffice List, 174–176, 186
    See also Address Book
Postoffice Manager dialog box
    adding user accounts, 195
    backing up and restoring files,
        198–199
    compressing files, 198
    deleting user accounts, 197
    information on shared folders,
        197–198
    modifying user accounts, 196–197
    opening personal mailboxes,
        172–173
    See also Workgroup Postoffice
PostScript printers, 154
Print dialog box, Schedule+, 233–234
Print Manager, 47
    browsing network printers, 150–152
    changing access to shared printers,
        134–135
    Connect Network Printer dialog
        box, 112, 151–154, 155–156
    connecting to printers, 150–154
    designating shared printers, 129–132

Index

quitting, 133–134
setting up network printers, 154–156
Share Printer dialog box, 131–132
viewing and canceling printing, 133–134
Printer menu
Connect Network Printer command, 112, 151
Disconnect Network Printer command, 156
Printers
assigning parallel port number to, 150, 151–152
browsing, 150–152
changing access to, 134–135
connecting to, 150–154
designating, 129–132
disconnecting from, 156
displaying users of, 125–127
enabling/disabling sharing, 100, 141
naming, 131, 148
network design and, 63
passwords for, 131–132
pathnames for, 121, 152
requirements for, 85
setting up, 154–156
sharing, 7–8, 129–135
sharing at startup, 132, 153
viewing and canceling document printing, 133–134
Printers dialog box, 154–155
Printers function, Control Panel, 48
PRINTERS.WRI file, 154
Printing
Appointment Book, 233–234, 235
mail, 188
Task List, 233–234, 236
viewing and canceling, 133–134
Processors, network design and, 61

Program Information Files (PIF), 86
Program Manager
application window, 22–23
exiting Windows, 57
File menu, 38–39
Help system, 55
Window menu, 39
Program–item icons, 86
Programs. *See* Applications
Properties dialog box, 248–249
Protocols, for network interface cards, 68
Prt Sc key, 135, 136

Q

Quitting
Mail application, 188
Print Manager, 133–134
Schedule+, 222–223
Setup program, 93
Windows for Workgroups, 57

R

RAM. *See* Memory
ReadMe application, 47, 88, 95, 116
Read–only access, 120, 124–125, 139
Recurring Appointment dialog box, 219–221
Recurring Task dialog box, 227–228
Reminders, 221–222
Remote boot PROM, 75
Resource sharing. *See* Shared resources
Resources, scheduling, 243–244
Restore button, 29
Restore option, Control menu, 43
Restoring, Postoffice files, 199

Ring topology, 14–15
Root directory, 121, 144

S

Save Attachment dialog box, 191
Schedule+, 47, 206–244
    access privileges for others, 234–237
    accessing others' schedules, 237–238
    arranging meetings, 208–209,
        240–242
    Help, 209–211
    Mail and, 208–209, 211–212
    menu bar, 212
    other scheduling programs and,
        238–241
    quitting, 222–223
    scheduling resources, 243–244
Schedule+ Appointment Book
    adding appointments, 214–219
    Assistant user for, 242–243
    changing defaults, 213–214
    exporting/importing appointments,
        238–239
    opening, 211–212
    overview of, 206–207
    printing, 233–234, 235
    recurring appointments, 219–221
    reminders, 221–222
    Schedule+ Planner and, 208–209,
        240–242
    Task List and, 231–232
    tentative appointments, 221
Schedule+ Planner, 208–209, 240–242
Schedule+ Task List
    adding tasks, 223–228
    Appointment Book and, 231–232
    deleting tasks, 230
    moving and copying tasks, 228–229

    overview of, 207–208, 223
    printing, 233–234, 236
    recurring tasks, 226–228
    viewing and sorting tasks, 229–230
Scheduling software, 10–11
    Schedule+ and, 238–241
Screens, startup, 22–24
Scroll bars, 31–33
Scroll option, Control menu, 44
Security, 8, 98
    See also Access privileges; Passwords
Select Attendees dialog box, 240–241
Select Computer dialog box, 159,
    244–245
Send Note dialog box, 177–178
Send Request dialog box, 241–242
Servers, 4, 7, 12
Set Access Privileges dialog box,
    234–237
Settings option, Control menu, 44
Setup program, 47, 86–95
    AUTOEXEC.BAT and, 87, 88–89
    CONFIG.SYS and, 87, 88, 89
    copying files from, 115–116
    Custom Setup, 91–93
    Express Setup, 90–91, 93
    installing Windows for
        Workgroups, 93–95
    quitting, 93
    tasks performed by, 86–87
    upgrading from Windows 3.0 to
        3.1, 87–88
    See also Troubleshooting
SETUP.TXT, 102–103
Share ClipBook Page dialog box,
    137–139
Share Directory dialog box, 123–125,
    195
Share Printer dialog box, 131–132

Index

Shared Folders dialog box, 198
Shared resources, 119–141
   displaying users of, 125–127
   enabling/disabling, 100, 141
   explained, 119–120
   Net Watcher and, 125, 133, 247–249
   passwords and, 120, 125
   pathnames and, 121
   shared databases, 10
   stopping sharing, 129, 134–135,
      140, 141
   WinMeter and, 249–250
   See also ClipBook; Directories;
      Printers
Shells, 16
Shielded twisted–pair cables, 67
[Shift] key
   + [F1] key (Help), 55
   + [Tab] key (navigating with), 42
   selecting files with, 51
Shortcut keys, 39, 41–42
   See also [Alt] key; [Ctrl] key; [Shift] key
Single–user software, 9, 10
16–bit network interface cards, 68–69,
   70, 72
Size option, Control menu, 43
Slots, network interface cards and,
   68–69
SMARTDRV.EXE command, 88, 89
Software
   network, 3, 9–11
   network operating systems, 16–17
   requirements, 84–85
Sound cards, 85
Sound function, Control Panel, 49
[Spacebar], 42, 43
Standard mode
   versus 386 enhanced mode, 95–96
   resource sharing and, 143–144

system requirements for, 85
Star topology, 14–15, 64–65, 66
Startup screen, 22–24
Static electricity, 70
Stop Sharing Directory dialog box, 129
Stop Sharing Printer dialog box,
   134–135
Switch To option, Control menu, 43
Switches, network interface card,
   71–72
System requirements, 13, 84–85

T

[Tab] key, 42
Task dialog box, 223–224, 226
Task List. *See* Schedule+ Task List
Technical support, 116–117
Tee connectors, 66, 77
Telephone cable, 67
Templates, mail, 188–189
Tentative appointments, 221
Terminals, multiuser systems and, 3
Terminators, 64, 77, 103
Thick/Thin Ethernet cables, 69
386 Enhanced function, 48
386 enhanced mode
   Net Watcher and, 247
   sharing resources in, 120
   versus standard mode, 95–96
   system requirements for, 85
   troubleshooting, 110–111
   WinMeter and, 249
Thumbnails option, 54
Time function, Control Panel, 48
Time management. *See* Schedule+
Title bar, 22
Toolbar, ClipBook Viewer, 157–158
Topologies, 14–15, 64–65

Trees, star topology and, 64
Troubleshooting, 79–81, 102–117
   386 enhanced mode, 110–111
   AUTOEXEC.BAT file, 104
   cables, 81, 103
   CD–ROM drives, 113
   computer lockups, 106–107
   computers do not appear, 112–113
   CONFIG.SYS file, 104
   Connect dialog box, 112–113
   device drivers, 108
   floppy drives, 108
   hardware, 79–81, 103–106
   memory managers and, 80
   memory–resident programs, 109
   mouse, 114–115
   network adapter driver, 105
   network features, 111–112
   network interface cards, 79–81, 103–106
   passwords, 112
   setup problems, 102–117
   SETUP.TXT for, 102–103
   technical support for, 116–117
   terminators, 103
   Windows won't start, 109–110
   Workgroup Postoffice, 201–202
TSRs. *See* Memory–resident software
Twisted–pair cables, 66–68
   ARCnet cards and, 70
   versus coaxial cables, 68
   Ethernet cards and, 69
286 computers, 143–144

U

Underscore character (_), 115
Upgrading, from Windows 3.0 to 3.1, 87–88

Upper memory. *See* Memory
Users
   Appointment Book Assistant, 242–243
   displaying, 125–127
Utility software, 11

View menu, 54
Virtual memory, 95

WANs (Wide Area Networks), 3
Window menu, Program Manager, 39
Windows, 28–41
   Accessories window, 33–37
   active, 24
   application, 22–23, 28–29
   closing, 57
   dialog boxes, 39–41
   document, 22–23, 28–29
   maximize button, 23, 29
   menus, 38–39
   minimize button, 23, 29
   moving, 29–31
   resizing, 29–31
   restore button, 29
   scroll bars, 31–33
   starting applications, 33–37
Windows program. *See* Microsoft Windows for Workgroups
WinMeter application, 249–250
Wireless LANs, 14
Workgroup Postoffice
   connecting to, 170–172
   deleting, 200

Index

versus Mail application, 193
moving, 200
on other networks, 200–201
overview of, 166–167
pathname for, 171
renaming, 199–200
setting up, 192–193, 202
sharing, 194–195
troubleshooting, 201–202
See also Mail application
Workgroup Postoffice administrator,
   192–200
adding user accounts, 195–196
backing up and restoring files,
   198–199
compressing files, 198
deleting user accounts, 197

information on shared folders,
   197–198
modifying user accounts, 196–197
modifying Workgroup Postoffice,
   199–200
overview of, 166
setting up, 193–194
Workgroups
defined, 3, 10
naming, 100
Workspace, 23
Workstations
client, 4–5, 12
defined, 5
diskless, 104
peer–to–peer, 12–13